SHOLA ADEWALE SANDY

ICE

I Can Explain

Challenging the power and abuse of a headteacher and their allies

To my father, *Alhaji Rafiu Omokayode Adewale*

It would have made you so proud to see your name in print, thank you for inspiring me by showing by example, that anything is possible……if you work hard at it!

'You are truly missed!'

Your daughter, *Shola*

First published in Great Britain in 2022

Copyright © Shola Adewale Sandy

The moral right of this author has been asserted.

All rights reserved.

No part of this publication may be reproduced, stored in a retrieval system, or transmitted, in any form or by any means, without the prior permission in writing of the publisher, nor be otherwise circulated in any form of binding or cover other than that in which it is published and without a similar condition including this condition being imposed on the subsequent purchaser.

Editing, design, typesetting and publishing by UK Book Publishing

www.ukbookpublishing.com

ISBN: 978-1-915338-48-8

Contents

Biography ii

Acknowledgments iii

Thursday June 4th, 2020 1

Saturday June 6th, 2020 27

Sunday June 7th, 2020 46

Tuesday June 9th, 2020 75

Thursday June 11th 2020 92

Friday June 12th, 2020 117

Saturday June 13th, 2020 139

Sunday June 14th 2020 164

Monday June 15th, 2020 187

Tuesday June 16th 2020 213

Friday June 19th 2020 242

Biography

Shola is an enthusiastic secondary school Mathematics Teacher, who loves to see the magic that happens in her lessons, when one of her students say, "*Yes, Miss, I finally get it now!*"

Shola is the proud author of the debut novel called 'ICE, the trilogy' which stands for *I Can Explain*, it's her memoirs that follows her journey in the educational system as a professional black woman and the importance of stopping systematic discrimination, that unfortunately she has experienced and witnessed over a decade, working in inner London schools.

She is also the co-founder of *Camp Evolution*, which is a residential camp for children aged 9 to 17. The camp focuses on key personal developmental areas and equips young people with a holistic understanding of themselves and others, as they start to make decisions about their future.

In her spare time, when Shola is not marking books, she loves to read autobiographies, dreams of being a cake taster on the show '*The Great British Bake Off*', and attempts for the 1000th time, to solve the Rubik's cube!

Shola happily lives with her family in East London, home of the Olympics.

Acknowledgements

Gosh, where do I start? I have been lucky enough and so blessed to have a solid group of people around me. When I said, "I am writing a book" you didn't blink or question me, even though I questioned myself. Thanking you all abundantly for your support, there are too many of you to mention…

Firstly, thank you God enormously for giving me the strength to go through that traumatic nightmare back then, and then over and over again in the process of writing, drafts, reading and editing this book. Making me be able to see it right through to the very end, against all the odds, I cannot thank you enough!

Hubby aka Bear, my rock and soulmate, you inspire me daily, thank you for supporting me through the ups and the many downs, giving me the space to breathe and most importantly believing in me.

To my mum, sisters and brother, we have been through so much as a family, may we see brighter days together, love you all immensely! And to my mother-in-law, thank you for your kind words and always checking up on me, also your unique delicious black cake, I appreciate that and you so much!

Thank you, Ezi, all of these years and I still pronounce your name in my own unique way! You believed in my project right from the very start, you made it your mission for me to actually live through the writing process and not just survive, by bringing spas, trips, dancing, food and so much joy into my life! Where would I be without you??

Debbie, what an example of a strong black woman you are! Not only that, but a true friend, who does not just walk the walk but talks the talk, I could not have done this without you! Reading and editing my manuscript repeatedly, I know has been traumatic for you, especially as you lived the nightmare with me all those years ago. May we finally see justice take place!

To Brother Robert, thank you for those delicious home cooked meals and your inspiring words really nourished my belly and my soul! Keep up the fight with your 'Black re-education 'shows!

Dolapo, thank you for taking my chunky manuscript to America and Turkey during the summer holidays, all so you could give me constructive feedback on my writing, also making your support available to me throughout, I truly appreciate it!

To Julie, all those takeaways were instrumental in me being able to focus on the job at hand, thank you for that and for always being there and believing in me over the years, a true friend and ally!

Ju, for being so inspirational when you went through the process yourself years ago, I now understand the madness of it all, also much appreciations for taking me on all those work trips, that really allowed me the time to heal and grow.

Nicola, my college friend who never forgets my birthdays or any other occasion, despite my years of protest, I appreciate all those cards,

ACKNOWLEDGEMENTS

candles, face masks and chilli sauce in your well wrapped packages! Thank you!

My long suffering Baptist high school crew, who put up with me talking about the book, over and over again in-between mouthfuls of pounded yam and ewedo soup on our many visits to Nigerian food joints, thanks for footing the bill, guys, on so many occasions, my round, next time!

My students, past, present and those not with us anymore, every day I get up just for you, you inspire me to do more and get better in conveying the joy and importance of Mathematics in life. (yes, I hear all the groans!) And most of all, being the best version of yourself, keep believing in you, because I certainly do!

To all my hardworking colleagues, past and present who have become friends, Sonia with your weekly Thursday texts, so inspiring, you don't know how much they motivated me to write, especially on those days when I could not string two words together, let alone write a sentence! Thank you, enormously!

Steve, what an educator, colleague and friend you are! I also love how you embrace life with both hands, despite your dedication to your job! Sometimes I wish I was one of your students, education is truly blessed that you chose it as a career. And Kemton, with your infectious laugh and your ability to bust serious jokes, you make the job a joy to do daily!

To my beautiful nephew, Seun and nieces, Victoria and Sarah, the world is your oyster, go grab it and live your best life! Love you all tremendously!

My gorgeous Godchildren, Emy, Ije, and Kerena, where does the time go? I never spent the time I needed to with you, I hope now you will understand why… I love you all so much and I know you will all go on to achieve great things!

A massive thank you to the team at UK Book Publishing – Ruth and Jay, you really took on this project and understood what I was trying to say with such flair! You did a really fantastic job!

And finally to my lovely readers, each and every one of you, thank you so much for buying and reading my book, you are making my dreams come true and most importantly you are part of change that we all welcome in 2022!

Thursday June 4th, 2020

"It's time for us to stand up in George's name and say, GET YOUR KNEE OFF OUR NECKS!" AL Sharpton, the civil rights activist, proclaimed passionately. All I could hear were those last six words over and over again in my head. There were claps of agreement and echoes resonating around the church among the congregation and directly to me, from across the Atlantic Ocean to good old Stratford in East London.

The first memorial was being streamed live on TV. I felt I was in the church with the rest of the congregation; all my senses were heightened. I truly felt I was present in mind, body and soul, wearing my face mask among family and friends. Giving my condolences to them with the many other supporters who had turned out to represent and support the family of the late George Floyd, aka 'Big Floyd', who was horrifically taken before his time.

I stood up in my living room, like the congregation had, and shouted out loud to no one in particular – why I was still awake, I can't remember, all I know is I was unsettled, but drawn to this broadcast.

"YEAH!... GET YOUR FRIGGING KNEE OFF MY NECK!" I felt the sound running through my bloodstream and veins from the tips of my overgrown cornrowed hair to my purple chipped toenails (don't judge me, people... it's lockdown!). It felt like I had been suddenly slapped round the head.

A slap that you used to get when you were younger, a slap I used to get from my Nigerian parents to let you understand what time it was, a slap that was so sudden, you forget to cry for those first few nano-seconds, because your body was in so much shock from the impact of the slap. This was so much deeper, at that moment I was jolted into the realisation and the picture that seemed blurred over the years slowly came into focus.

As I stood there and started to pace and circle the room, breathing fast and my mind racing through all the situations that I have witnessed and been in, something came over me at that moment; I felt pins and needles throughout my body. It was like at that precise point in time, I had a jolt, a reckoning, a realisation.

I finally realised that I have had a knee firmly on my neck for over the last decade and it took the great AL Sharpton to break it down and put it the best way with words I could never find or utter before. I have not been able to breathe properly all this time, and I did not understand that then but it made sense now – what a relief to finally diagnose the problem, or should I say illness, that has been in the background choking me of life all these years.

It's the early hours of the morning and I am watching black people come out and talk about their lived experiences. It is everywhere on all news channels, social media and radio. I am immersed in it all: is this really our moment for change?

How can I process how I feel? As they have been suppressed for so long, so much delayed grief within me without identifying what it was?

How can I begin to breathe properly – I have had someone's knee on my neck indirectly for years? I ask myself, as tears fall down my face. Now I understand.

Not only were my feelings on another level, most people's emotions, in my opinion were enhanced at this point in history due to this Covid-19 thing that was affecting everyone's lives worldwide, rich or poor, black or white.

People were either losing or not being able to see loved ones because of all of the restrictions and the fear of passing the virus on to them. People were losing their jobs and experiencing real poverty. Businesses were struggling and, in some cases, going bust. It felt at that moment that people of all races around the world were waking up and indeed smelling the coffee, especially in the black community as we seem to be affected the most by this damn virus!

Around 2012, 'The Black Lives Matter' movement was formed, galvanising in speed each time another life is lost in the black community at the hands of the police. Not surprising when the news broke out that Breonna Taylor, an innocent black lady was shot eight times by armed police in her own home on March 13th, 2020. The black community and our allies were out on the street once again asking for justice for the family and fairness in the system.

And this reaction was the same when the video of George Floyd's murder began to go viral on social media. Even more so as this was the first time for many watching what the black community have been going through for years and now it was out there and available for all to see clearly all over the world. This was real, happening in the Western world where we were supposed to be civilised to one another. It was just so shocking. For me personally, I still cannot put into words how I felt when I caught a glimpse of that video and heard a snitch of the audio.

I can't watch the entire video of George Floyd's murder in Minneapolis that took place that evening on the 25th of May 2020.

I really don't give two hoots why he was arrested; all I know is that he was not resisting arrest. He seemed to be claustrophobic so was having trouble getting into the vehicle. This escalated to George being on the ground with one of the officers' knee on his neck. George kept saying he could not breathe, but it seemed the policeman was not listening to him or to the bystanders who kept telling Derek Chauvin, the policeman, to get off George's neck.

"Can't you see he can't breathe!" the bystanders repeatedly said.

"I can't breathe," George repeatedly said.

For eight minutes 46 seconds, Derek Chauvin had his knee on Mr George Floyd's neck with his hand causally in his pocket. This was a father of five, someone's son, brother, uncle and friend, a human being with the same red blood running through his veins on the ground, dying as each second passed.

Derek Chauvin, I later found out, was the most senior of the four police officers present. He acted as the judge, jury and executioner of an incident that day that ultimately ended George's life in less than nine minutes.

What amazes me about this is the fact that Derek Chauvin and his colleagues knew they were being filmed and choose to continue to stand by watching all this unfold and do absolutely nothing.

The day after George Floyd's death, the Minneapolis Police department fired all four police officers involved, but it took three days of protest, demonstrations and marches in absolute outrage that something more needed to be done to all the police officers concerned. Especially the lead man Derek, otherwise known as the "Slow assassinator". The protests started peacefully but became ugly as fires were started up and there was looting in the local shops. The police attempted to disperse the crowds with rubber bullets and tear gas, which only frustrated the protesters more.

Finally, the people above must have been listening and witnessing what was happening in towns across America and of course around the world. They realised they would have to be seen to be doing much more. Thankfully, on May 29th of 2020, Derek Chauvin was finally arrested and charged with third-degree murder and second-degree manslaughter. He had faced 17 misconduct complaints over the course of his 19-year career, we later found out – can you imagine?

THURSDAY JUNE 4TH, 2020

Seventeen misconduct complaints, really? And he was still employed by the police. Trust me, if that was a person of colour, I really do not think they would have remained in that role, let alone still be employed by the organisation.

***

The first few nights that followed the death of George Floyd the streets were filled with anger and cries for justice. By day there were Black Lives Matter marches and protesters in parks all over the world. In the UK we listened to passionate speeches by activists and respected members from the black community through the news. Even though the government had said no gatherings due to the Covid-19 outbreak, the protesters thought this issue was far too important and had to come out and make a stand, regardless of the pandemic. To be fair, the majority of protesters were wearing face masks and trying to social distance.

In one particular protest inside one of London's famous parks, John Boyega, the black actor from *'Star Wars'*, my Nigerian brother, spoke from the heart that day, not caring whether he would have any type of career after his moving speech. I could feel his emotional words and message travel across the airways straight into my heart, hoping that him telling his truth would not affect him in a negative way in the future.

Ashley Walters, the gentleman behind the gritty drama *'Top Boy'*, gave an eye-opening account on social media of what he had gone through in his life in regards to racism and police brutality. It was so raw. I felt I could relate to the pain he was feeling. Holding it down and trying to make a success of his life despite what he had gone through. Rising above what would have been expected of him and staying focused on his goals.

Even Oprah, an influential person globally, had been fighting racism over the years. Probably, in her frustration at the lack of progress, she had an amazing TV programme in which she was trying to find solutions with a wealth of accomplished black people. Coming from a range of professions joining her together virtually on Zoom to voice their opinions and say their truths.

Hearing all these testimonials made me recap all those incidents in which I was made to feel less than over the years. It was quite emotional for me to watch, hear and process how I was feeling.

***

During the first few weeks of lockdown, it felt like I was seeing ambulances constantly whizzing past me with their flashing lights and loud sirens rushing to and from the local hospitals, no doubt carrying patients suffering from this virus. I had witnessed the Nightingale hospital being put together to get ready for the thousands of patients it was expecting. It was amazing the speed in which it was constructed. You would never believe it was the Excel conference centre in East London that was famously used for events such as marathons and science-fiction conventions. Now it specialised in dealing with the predicted surge from patients who had contracted Covid-19.

Just watching the ventilators and the heavy-duty equipment being wheeled in, kept me constantly worried and the nation on high alert about the centre being used and how many patients would actually walk out of there alive.

Human nature is so amazing! There were call outs for professional staff to volunteer at this new hospital and other emergency hospitals being built all around the country. Calling people to come out of retirement even, more than 250,000 volunteers were needed – can you imagine, the nerve?

And to my amazement, the quota was over-filled. Indeed, those special people came out to fill those roles to help other people during this dire time, truly amazing!

There were moments of distraction and joy, like doing my daily allowed hour of exercise. Walking in my local area and seeing the beautiful drawn rainbow pictures on the windows of my neighbours' houses and on the pavements. Knowing that my neighbours would have created them lovingly in appreciation of the NHS. Or me listening to Fleur East, an East London singer, who had that catchy charity track about Covid-19, 'Not Alone'. You could not help bobbing your head too, smiling at her lyrical jokes, knowing the money raised for the purchase of the single was going to the NHS.

Nature had a chance to recuperate too. No one was flying anywhere unless it was an emergency, thus there were fewer planes in the sky. It seemed the birds took ownership of the skies, with louder and richer bird song, especially in the early mornings.

Pollution was less in the air so we could breathe and see the stars. The rivers and some animals that were nearly extinct got a chance to revive and blossom. We were even driving less, as we were encouraged to stay and work from home, if possible. I even got a reasonable refund on my car insurance during that period – can you imagine, who would have ever thought an insurance company would ever be giving me a refund?

And what about 99-year-old Captain Tom who decided to walk 100 laps of his garden to raise £100 for his 100th birthday, initially as a family joke. The money was for the NHS to thank them for the assistance he had received when he had a hip replacement. Watching him go back and fro in his garden using his Zimmer frame became a familiar feature on the news.

The money raised escalated to £1,000, getting nationwide attention, then to £100,000 and then started to hit the millions as his story travelled around the world. It was absolutely amazing watching the fund grow in front of our very eyes as his birthday finally approached. What was truly amazing is that he inspired so many other people to fundraise, from the older generation to youngsters.

Captain Tom received more than 160,000 birthday cards, from admirers and well-wishers from all around the world! The local post office was so overwhelmed, that a decision was made to display the cards in a nearby school hall; the visual effect was amazing! All the varied sizes of cards covered the walls and floor with a blaze of colour and handwritten inspirational messages that were so moving. The final money raised was more than £33 million and he went on to achieve further accolades, totally unbelievably!

On the 2nd of June, it was termed 'Black out Tuesday'. It was started by Brianna Agyemang and Jamila Thomas, based in the US, who are employed by Atlantic Records. They released a powerful statement, that asked people in the music industry and wider relatable corporations to basically take a stand for the contribution that black people have made to the industry. Music celebrities took this on and it manifested in them posting black squares on their social media platforms or going quiet on the day or just simply sharing the statement.

I could not believe this was happening! Companies that wanted to show solidarity with the Black Lives Matter movement showed this by blacking out their Social media pages. I was actually watching 'Good Morning' on ITV with presenters Holly and Phil coming across as being really authentic. They announced that they would be blacking out their screens to support the movement and indeed a few moments later my screen went black with just the text across it, 'Black Lives Matter'. Absolutely powerful for me to witness this on mainstream TV in the UK. I was brought to tears, with the efforts people were making.

People were taking responsibility and doing research, asking those uncomfortable questions, having those over-due discussions and seeing ways to move forward together as one human race.

Books from black writers in the UK and USA were flying off the shelf. In fact, nine out of 15 books on The New York best seller list were written by black writers, unbelievable but true!

Even big corporations like Netflix, Coca-Cola, Lego and Google just to name a few are wanting to address injustices by putting millions of pounds into black-owned businesses. Hopefully, to deal with the inequalities those businesses face on a daily basis. Let's hope they stay true to their word; "We will be watching oh!" (in Nigerian dialect)

In the UK, marches continued in big cities and small rural communities, even in villages. The Black Lives Matter movement were demonstrating in more than 50 countries including Tokyo, Japan and all over East Asia. In China the death of George Floyd was condemned, but just in April of this year, a city in China had displayed written signs forbidding black people from entering shops and restaurants, apparently to stop the spread of Covid-19.

Some African residents there, supposedly have been evicted from their homes and experienced signs of violence. I was shocked that this was allowed to happen, but unfortunately, many countries have to deal with the racism and systemic discrimination in their communities, despite how far I thought we had ALL come as a human race.

Taking the knee has been in our history as a form of saying a statement, without verbally saying it. The first known image was of an enslaved black man, kneeling chained by the hands and feet in the 1780s with a scroll along the bottom of the image saying,

'Am I not a man and a brother'

Martin Luther King did it too, back on the 1st of February in 1965 during a prayer outside the Dallas County Alabama Courthouse. In recent years, a baseball player called Chris Kaepernick did it during the National Anthem before a game to protest about the discrimination within the National Football League(NFL). The image went viral around the world, it started a storm because his president (you know who!) did not approve. From then on, more and more sports celebrities joined in and this continued in several countries. I remember I wanted to do it myself at the school I worked in then, but we will get into that further on in the book.

Later that day, many organisations took the knee. Even Sir Keir Starmer, the Labour party leader, did it in public, which was a symbolic gesture that I personally really appreciated.

During this time even police officers were taking the knee, while on the front line. What a powerful image! I imagined being an officer on that front line, listening to all the abuse and feeling all that anger and distress, as you stand there proudly in your uniform, trying to put aside your personal feelings and concentrate on the job at hand. Let's not even try to imagine being a black officer at this time in history.

The first and only black Chief Constable was on the media recently; he had just released his book:

'Kill the black one first'

What a title, I thought, I can't imagine having to go through my career always looking over my shoulder, when all I was trying to do was my job.

"You sell out!" I heard some protesters shouting at the black officers that were on the front line. What were those police officers supposed to do? They had to pay bills like the rest of us!

But really, what were they supposed to do? if that was me, I would be taking my annual leave right about now, do they or don't they take the knee while on duty? I would want to be supported whatever decision I make.

As the evening progressed, it began to get ugly and arrests were made. Some say that those were radical protesters and were not really part of the movement. Some say people felt years of anger and frustration coming to the forefront and there was no outlet, whether it was right or wrong is hard to say; on the one hand I hated seeing their local communities where they live being burned up and destroyed, and on the other, I understood the principle of why they were out there.

On Wednesday the 3rd of June, there were more protests. In fact, thousands gathered in Hyde Park. It was organised by a group called 'Justice for Black lives' led by a young activist called Naomi who managed to pull it together in just three days!

A more serious charge of second-degree murder was added in the case against Derek Chauvin. The other three officers were charged with aiding and abetting second-degree murder.

The question is, would this have happened so swiftly if the protesters were not so highly visible and verbal?

People say why are you so worked up? You don't even live in America!

Why does this affect you? It's not the same here, police don't carry guns! That may be true, but we do have a history of police brutality and institutional racism within the police force here. All this violence I was witnessing was very worrying for me as I have close family members and friends over there.

In the early 90s, I worked in Minneapolis with my good friend Amanda for a well-known children's residential holiday camp. We worked intensely for a few months, taking on any extra shifts, which gave us the opportunity to save as much money as possible and travel around some of the states. We reached as far as Texas and Florida, using Amtrak and Greyhound to get us around and surviving on lukewarm pot noodles and tasteless skimmed milk. It was one of the best summers of my life. The local people in each state embraced us, letting us into their homes and showing us around their beautiful cities and suburbs; we were truly humbled by their generosity and hospitality.

As soon as your British accent was heard, you would be asked the same few typical questions: *"Would you like a cup of tea?"* with the best English accent they could fathom, or *"Do you know the Queen?"*;

also *"Why do you guys always talk about the weather?"*. We would laugh and answer politely.

We were offered discounts in shops and given VIP treatment wherever we went, we were even able to jump the queue at clubs. Don't ask me why the British accent went down so well, but we did not complain! Anyway, I think fondly of Minneapolis often, even more so now as it was in the middle of this global incident.

After, I calmed down by practising the breathing techniques that I had got from my counsellor years ago, I remembered a phone call I had received just the other day from a dear friend and former employer who just so happens to be white.

Dr Ju was an intelligent woman and a whiz on the computer. I think she was the first one to hand in her thesis online in the UK. She was an academic, model, author and a disability activist. Having those two letters before her name immediately gave her some level of respect, which in my opinion she deserved.

She reminded me of Annie Lenox, the famous female singer from the group *'Eurythmics'*, with similar sharp features and her focused demeanour. I have worked with her on and off as a Personal Assistant and I considered her more of a friend than an employer.

Ring ring

Dr Ju: How are you coping in these times, Shola, I was wondering whether you could do with some masks and gloves, as I have a few spares.

Me: That would be great, when can I pick them up?

Dr Ju: I will pop them in a bag by the gate, also I will put in a letter, just in case you are stopped by the police. Let me know if you want me to email it to you instead.

I laughed as I knew what she meant! I did not have to explain to her the trickiness of the situation, she had lived in Newham for years and was aware of how people of colour were treated. Ju was familiar with the system and the high proportion of us being stopped by the police.

Me: Do you need anything yourself, hun?

At the time, the madness of the toilet tissue saga was ongoing and supermarkets' queues were out of the car park with a one to two hour wait. She had been quarantined at home for the past nine weeks as she had underlying health conditions; even the waiting list for home delivery for disabled people was weeks long.

Dr Ju: Some soya milk would be good, as I am running low.

Me: Cool, will pick some up, when I am doing my shopping, hopefully they will have some in stock.

Dr Ju: I will text you when the letter is ready.

With the rules at the time being do not leave your house unless going for food, work or your one hour of exercise, she knew I would likely be stopped by the police to ask me what and where I was going. Having a letter to say I had a legitimate reason to be out from a doctor, carrying out key worker duties would allow me to drop her soya milk off and pick the masks up without worrying about the journey and justification for being on the road.

After all, black people were four times more likely to be stopped during this lockdown period. The government advice was don't use public transport unless necessary. People were encouraged to use their cars or other forms of transport to get to and from work.

If everyone acted this way and tried to live in our shoes the world would indeed be a better place. I was associating words with her thoughts and actions like *'ally'* and *'anti-racist'*. I remember at the time pausing at the end of the call and appreciating her even more for understanding the situation and thinking of solutions that would work for me. Understanding her position as a white person and using that to help me, when she really didn't have to. Ju was using her *'White privilege'* for good.

But, a great example of someone taking advantage of their *'White privilege'* happened on the 26th May 2020. An African American man called Christian Cooper was in Central Park in New York, he was minding his business, watching birds and taking pictures. A women called Amy Cooper (no relation to each other) had her dog running around, scaring the birds. He asked her to please put her dog on the leash, she refused to do this and then threatened to call the police on him – can you imagine!

Lo and behold, to my amazement she called 911, her voice changed, all of a sudden, she was sounding highly distressed. You would never believe it was the same person!

"There is a man, African American, he has a bicycle helmet, he is recording me and threatening me and my dog!"

She went on to say, *"I am being threatened by a man in the Ramble, please send the cops immediately."* She then finally fixes a leash to the dog's collar in anticipation of the police's arrival.

Mr Cooper did not seem fazed by the call; if anything, he remained calm and kept a steady hand as he was filming the whole thing on his camera. He said afterwards he was accustomed to this type of treatment.

Thank God when the police arrived, it was deemed a verbal dispute. Can you imagine what would have happened if the police had aggressively approached the situation. Guess who would have ended up on the ground, with a knee on his neck, mouthing the words

'I can't breathe'!

Thankfully, soon afterwards Amy Cooper was fired from the investment firm Franklin Templeton that she worked for. At least she can go onto some sort of acting career, if anyone will give her that opportunity. Thank you, Franklin Templeton, for doing the right thing as a company!

**

But really, what if I could have a conversation with a few of my past colleagues, bosses or potential past employers to talk about how they made me feel? Now we all have had time to reflect with different people of colour coming forward, celebrities and non-celebrities speaking their truths. We have TV shows, podcasts, radio interviews and events dedicated to the black person's experiences, footballers, entertainers, academics, saying 'Systematic racism' has to stop. This seems to be the time for real meaningful change.

On reflecting on the conversation I had had with Ju, my mind started to race…

What if there was a system like the government's *Test and Trace app*? A system that could connect people that you have worked or associated with in the past. The Test and Trace system was first piloted in the Isle of Wight, a beautiful island in the UK, chosen probably because of the contained nature of its location. Some other countries have been really effective with 'Test and Trace', for example Hong Kong and New Zealand, all to benefit their community.

The Isle of Wight pilot wasn't as successful as planned. We were told by the government to expect a *'World beating service'*. We hope as more versions roll out over the UK over time, the imperfections will hopefully be ironed out and more people will trust and download the app to make it more accurate.

What if, just for a moment, instead of using it to find the people you have come into contact with to let them know you have the virus and for them to get tested and isolate, it's used instead to identify the people you have worked with in the past. Thereafter, you can request their number and the app sends you it automatically, so you can have a confidential conversation through the encrypted method.

Think about it for a moment: we all have mobile phones with our number; each time we upgrade we keep the sim card and change the phone itself but not the number. I have had my number since 1998, with various models of phones in that time and most of my friends have had the same number too for years. Our phones are linked to our names and addresses. Back in the day the home phone number had to be given before you worked anywhere, just to check you were legit. Maybe not so much now; either way, any number attached to your name is a simplified way of looking for persons of interest, especially now if you have a contract, which the majority of employed people do.

This information is available online directly with the phone companies, so the app would work in collaboration with them and Google, with the government doing the administration. All types of phones like the iPhone, Apple and Android phones would be able to access the app.

Some industries would include Education, Police, Hospitality, Security, IT, Health, Construction and Transport. It would cover a period of approximately 30 years, split into seven-year chunks to fit into a four-week period this app would run for.

This would be an opportunity for white, black, Asian, Chinese, whoever, to reflect and readdress their views and actions. Watching that video of George Floyd being murdered, left in everyone's minds that this simply could not be right. A lot of people were trying to see how they could right their wrongs, thinking of experiences that they had gone through and stopping to reflect on those incidents. Maybe, just maybe I might have offended someone, how can I resolve it? Is what I thought would be going through their minds.

This was a great idea; I am starting to feel better already!

I would call it **ICE**, the 'I Can Explain' app, effectively allowing people to communicate and have those conversations that should have been had but had never happened because of how hard it is to confront certain issues. This space would be neutral, you would have the right to refuse a call, but when you do accept a call, a constructive conversation had to be had from both sides and goals reached at the end of the talk.

Privacy is highly important, as some people might be vulnerable in that space, so it would be like WhatsApp, where conversations are encrypted and can be erased, but there would be a record that a call was made and received, so future generations can see whether their ancestors took up this golden opportunity when they had the chance to try to right their wrongs. It really was a moral decision, a way to show empathy and step outside of your space into the space of those affected.

All government departments would work together to connect establishments with industry and create a database of identifying people just with their personal mobile phone number.

A massive government centralised campaign would be galvanised and splattered on ALL media platforms and direct to individual people's phones, whatever brand, all synced to the system that will be launched this week.

1990 - 1996	Week 1(4th - 10th June 2020)	Childcare, Social Care, Police, Security
1997 - 2003	Week 2(11th - 17th June 2020)	Public Services: NHS, Transport
2004 - 2010	Week 3(18th - 24th June 2020)	Judicial system
2011 - 2017	Week 4(25th - 31st June 2020)	Public Services: HR, Education
Any year	Week 5(1st - 4th July 2020)	Any industry

The app would be free, of course, but compulsory, it would be available from the App store or Google play. If for some reason it does not automatically download to your phone, you will be able to scan a QR code from shop windows like our trusted post offices, barbers, nail salons and hairdressers. This was the government's way of trying to do something to affect the inequality of the nation and in some way try to address injustices of the past, by throwing a lot of resources and money into this project to promote the conversation.

To be honest, not everyone would be covered by this scheme: some people were self-employed or worked abroad. For the purposes of this book, we will assume all relevant people are resident in the UK, employed and have a phone with a contract. If you had mentioned this scheme to me last year, I would have laughed and said 'No way, Jose! It simply isn't possible', but we are living in different times now.

Furlough was a term I had never heard of before, using Zoom, Skype, Microsoft Teams to socialise and celebrate special occasions was something I had not really considered before like many others. If you had said to me last year we would all be wearing masks and using sanitiser like water, I would have said 'Never!' but look now, the majority of us are complying!

Think about it, would we have considered the thought of social distancing last year? Attending theatres, cinemas, clubs, swimming pools and libraries are a luxury now and some of those venues are closed at this present time. Having to self-isolate now when you test positive, as an adult is something else we have had to get our heads around, but it's deemed normal behaviour now.

The world population has had to get used to it while we wait patiently for a vaccine.

To be honest, how many people of colour were going through some sort of trauma, after seeing this type of vision over and over again, watching our black men being treated worse than animals, whether guilty or not. Therapy waiting lists were getting longer and longer, as people of colour wanted to talk about their experiences. This type of intervention by the government might go a long way and for me specifically, it would be some form of closure for what I went through, and I would feel finally acknowledged as a human being and not insignificant as I have done in the incidents I will share with you in this book.

The new series of Issa Rae 'Insecure' has finally come over to the UK after being shown first in the States; I was itching to watch it. Series 1-3 were so captivating, I already liked her after reading her book *'Awkward black girl'*. It was so refreshing watching normal black, beautiful, intelligent women going through stuff that all of us feel and have experienced. The clothing, hairstyles, dialogue and relationships, as well as it being filmed actually in Harlem was like taking a vacation in the middle of the day. I have laughed, cried and shouted out at so many of the scenarios that the girls get themselves into in the show.

My treat after going through all this heart wrenching stuff, recalling how people made me feel less than shit. I could not wait to finish and binge on the WHOLE series surrounded by wine, pandemic style pizza, double chucky chocolate cookies, tissues and true friends at the end of the telephone line to discuss.

Once you launch the app on your phone, it's a simple process. Write the name of the person and the industry, also roughly what year your paths might have crossed, and it will cross reference your number with people that fall into that category at that time. Once it narrows it down, the app will automatically send the number to you and then you have a window during that week to call up that person to have THAT conversation.

I personally would have downloaded the app expecting those people who have had time to reflect on having their knee on my neck on what they might have done differently given their time again. It would be like going back in a time machine!

Lastly, no one would be forced to make a call and of course you actually would not have to answer the call. But I expect decent human beings would want to do the right thing when given an opportunity.

At this point, you the reader should take the time to reflect, whatever side you are on. I have added some lined paper at the back of this book to give you the opportunity to write those names down and find a way to contact them to have 'that conversation'.

Let's be honest, in this day and age, it's not hard to track people down, searching up online or on social media. Someone might come to mind during the precious time you are taking to read my truth so do it then instead if you choose, just do it, don't let this opportunity pass you by. Trust me, you will feel much better afterwards for reaching out, however the conversation goes.

**

Getting back to my story, I have been told that my voice sounds quite British, but I feel like I sound like a real local working-class EastEnders, "You alright, luv", "Blinking hell" and my favourite "Gordon Bennet"!

Several times my students in class would say, "Who is Gordon Bennet, Miss?" And then we would spend a few moments googling, discussing and of course laughing once we found out.

I have always loved working with children. I remember babysitting when I was around 11 or 12 in the local neighbourhood and earning £5 to £10. That was big money to me for 3-4 hours' work and you got to eat snacks that the parents left out for you while watching the TV programmes I liked without anyone fighting me over the channels, absolute heaven! Once I got paid, Mum would collect it promptly, placing it safely in her bra:

"Bless you, my daughter, I am saving it for you oh!" (in Nigerian dialect) as she patted her chest and that would be the last time I would see that money!

When I was in Waltham Forest College in Walthamstow, East London doing my A Levels, I worked as a nanny, for the Slacks, a lovely family with two girls and a boy. I mostly looked after the youngest child, Chris, the sweetest child you could have imagined. He was about seven and in primary school; the girls were older and in secondary school and more independent, or so they wanted me to believe. My role really was to look after them after school, making sure they completed their homework and after school activities before the parents came home in the evening.

The Slacks really supported me in my early college days and were a joy to work for, they treated me as part of the family. I remember I would be walking Chris back from school, happy to see him, greeting him with a smile, hug and kiss, chatting about the day, people around would be so confused as we seemed to bounce off of one another and laugh and joke as we made our way back home. The colour of our skin was opposite ends of the spectrum, but we behaved like mother and son!

I never felt less than – if only the rest of my working life was the same! We went on holiday together several times to Wales as a family, I was paid reasonably and given time to myself. I had the best time, even tried to surf, with no success! It was so sad when we both had to go our separate ways after several years. I imagine Chris as a mature man now, with his mousey brown hair and a long fringe over his blue eyes, most probably a bike-riding scientist with children of his own.

Anyway, I remember flicking through 'The Lady' at the time looking for a childcare role that did not require me to live in. This was a magazine that had lots of nanny vacancies for well-to-do families. I remember one role catching my eye, as the age of the children were just right, and I decided to call to show my interest.

Ring ring

Me: Morning Ms S, I am calling about the nanny vacancy, is it still available?

Nanny job: Yes, it is, do you have experience and references?

After I reeled off my experiences with children in various settings over the years, she took my details, gave me her address and told me to pop over the next day. She sounded pleasant enough. The job was to look after two children and by the sounds of it, she liked me already, the job was in the bag!

I remember dressing smart and preparing myself mentally for the interview, I checked out directions to her road on the A-Z; the closest station was Highgate. I made my way there with plenty of time to spare. As I approached the road, the houses became bigger and the front porches could fit at least four cars easily. The foliage surrounding the houses were well maintained, with large, tall trees lining both sides of the road; you could tell it was a real family middle class residential area.

I have worked with wealthy people before in Fulham and Sloane Square, both in West London, so I was not too fazed. I spotted the number on the double gated property and pressed the minicom on the side wall.

A lady answered, I could not make out whether it was the lady I had spoken to yesterday. I looked towards the house and could see the net moving on one of the big bay windows, but the front door and gate remained closed.

Me: Afternoon, I am here about the nanny job, I have an interview...

There was a brief silence and I positioned myself to push the side gate open once I heard the buzzer, but nothing; then I heard the same voice through the minicom saying:

Nanny job: Sorry, the job has been taken.

THURSDAY JUNE 4TH, 2020

I was a bit taken aback and thought maybe she had not heard me correctly.

Me: I spoke to Ms S and she told me to come by today for an interview.

Nanny job: As I said, the job has been taken.

I waited for her to expand or let me in, but there was just a silence. The big, heavy wooden front door remained closed.
Eventually I managed to summon up something and said,

Me: Ok then...thanks!

Thanks for nothing is what I really wanted to say, but I wanted to keep it professional.
Confused, I turned my back to walk back up the road towards the station, thinking "What just happened there?" I thought why couldn't she just phone me to save me the trip, why didn't she come out or let me in to tell me face-to-face? Why did the little conversation we had seem so aggressive?
Suddenly it came to me, she must have thought I was a white person because of my voice, she must have been in shock and disappointed when she saw me. I can imagine her saying, *"There is a bloody nigga outside my door, hell no way is she getting past the gate, let alone look after my children!"* Thankfully I got a job with a lovely French family soon after, so it was her loss!
Till this day, the way I felt then comes rushing back to me. The feeling of rejection, of course, the feeling of being judged and the feeling of not being treated like a human being.
I would hope with this app, she would think to call me by finding my number from the magazine, which for the purpose of this book

was registered. This is how I feel the conversation would go:

ICE app

Ring ring

The app is working, it's the 1st week and my first call; I am so excited to begin the conversations.

> **Ms S:** Evening, Shola, I don't know if you remember me, I can explain...
>
> **Me:** Of course I do! I was thinking of you the other day, especially how you made me feel...
>
> **Ms S:** When I caught sight of you that day when you came for the interview from behind the curtains in my living room, I remember my mind instantly thought, oh my God, she's black! But you didn't sound black when I spoke to you on the phone.
>
> **Me:** I know, I get that a lot!

We both laughed; that seemed to break the ice.

> **Ms S:** I was young, naive and had a young family, I didn't know what my friends and family would think, if I employed you and also how would it have looked, you out with my children in my local area?
>
> **Me**: I understand...

THURSDAY JUNE 4TH, 2020

Ms S: My daughter has since married a black man, an accountant, and I have two beautiful grandchildren, who I could not imagine living without!

Me: Congratulations! Doesn't time fly!

Ms S: Don't get me wrong I didn't welcome him initially with open arms, but my daughter loved him and if I didn't accept him, I would have lost my daughter forever.

There was a pause and I could sense how difficult it must have been for her to get her head around issues that had been festering in her for years, but bought to the forefront.

Ms S: I can't ever imagine living without her, so I had to confront my bias and that's taken me a while.

Me: To be honest with you, I hated the fact that you did not even see me face-to-face. You invited me to come to your home and you did not have the decency to even speak to me.

Ms S: That was so rude of me, I just saw your colour first and I didn't know what else to do?

Me: It's ok, if you didn't want to give me the job that's fine, it's just the way you went about it. Remember, I am a human being with feelings; it left me confused.

Ms S: I understand now...

I took a moment to take that in. She continued,

> **Ms S:** I apologise wholeheartedly; I should have treated you better. In fact, now my daughter is looking for a live-in Nanny and has seen CVs from a diverse group of individuals, so her kids can teach their children that people come in all shapes, sizes and colours and not to judge, unlike me and the way I behaved to you!

We both laughed uncomfortably, but there was a silent agreement.

> **Me**: You have done a great job raising your daughter, don't beat yourself up.

> **Ms S:** That means a lot to me coming from you.

There was a pause, all that needed to be said, was said now after all those years.

> **Me:** Apology accepted, Ms S, it means a lot to me that you remembered and picked up the phone to call me. I wish your daughter well and hope she finds someone that works for her and her family, thanks for calling!

Wow! That felt great, that's the kind of therapy I need!

Saturday June 6th, 2020

This was the second memorial and private viewing for George Floyd. It was held at Cape Fear Conference B Headquarters in his birth state of North Carolina.

It was a more private affair in comparison to the first memorial, even though hundreds of people where outside chanting his name.

"We keep talking, we keep talking, we keep talking until it happens again. ... Enough of talking. Don't let the life of George Floyd be in vain," said Hoke County Sheriff Hubert Peterkin.

***

Just yesterday on the 5th of June, due to the attention that the protesters were drawing to the White House in Washington DC, demonstrating on the street right in front of the house, known as 16th Street every night since the death of George Floyd. The Department for Public Works decided to repaint the road with the words 'Black Lives Matter' in bold yellow. It looked like a verbal and painful cry to the president across the road, asking for leadership and empathy during these times. The image was amazing, especially from the aerial cameras.

Afterwards I think the mayor decided to rename the street 'Black Lives Matter Plaza' and put up a new street sign to cement the change.

When she was interviewed by NBC Washington, she said: *"We want to call attention today to making sure our nation is more fair and more just, and that black lives and that black humanity matters in our nation."* You go, girl! your actions speak volumes and has been heard ALL around the world!

***

I was already emotional; we just had the last clap for carers on 28th of May which had run for 10 weeks on a Thursday at 8pm. The lady who started it in the UK was a yoga teacher called Ms Plas. What the key workers really wanted was for us to stay in our bloody homes, to get a pay rise and preferably a holiday when all this is done as they were absolutely exhausted.

I was banging my pots for all my friends working in the NHS, the nurses and doctors who had and continue to treat my friends and family in hospital. I was clapping for all the postmen as I could not have survived this pandemic without Amazon Prime (please feel free to give me free membership!).

***

A massive protest was being held in Parliament Square. Those attending were again from various backgrounds with a lot of white people coming out to show that they were not going to be silent anymore. There was singing, drumming, chanting 'No justice, no peace', all very peaceful and abiding by the government rules. The atmosphere seemed to be filled with energy, the desire for change, just like I felt approximately 10 years ago.

East London school

May 2006

Cover Supervisor – 2 posts

Scale 5 £17,337 to £18,880 – (inclusive of London Weighting)

36 hours per week-term time only – 39 weeks per year

Starting date to be agreed

Ref: ED 70559

You will need to have experience of working with 11-16-year olds. You will also need patience, a sense of humour and be able to work under pressure.

Your duties will be to cover registration, invigilate examinations, provide classroom support, to assist school trips with students, support school clubs, to provide administration support, mainly within designated subject areas.

A full CRB check will be carried out.

Closing date 8 June 2006

"Cover Supervisor?" That sounds like an interesting role, I said to myself, as I scanned the job adverts in the Newham Recorder in 2006. I focused on the advert. I thought, that sounds just like me, I can do this! The advert did not mention what subject area, but I would love to be in the Maths Department, I thought. Working in youth centres over the years and practically raising my 12-year-old nephew, I knew I had the skills required. I had been looking for experience in working in a school setting and this job had my name all over it! I remember thinking if I was lucky enough to get the job I would be over the moon. I saw it as a great opportunity to develop my skills, I hurriedly rang up for an application form to be sent to me, before the closing date.

Name: Shola Adewale, Age: 32 Marital Status: Miss, soon to be Mrs in approximately three months' time, to a lovely, gentle, giant man, named Bear. Sex: Female, even though I have been mistaken for a tomboy, because I tended to stay away from skirts and dresses, and cannot comfortably walk with heels for any amount of time unless I am being driven to and from my destination, must be because of my flat feet! I have been told that I inherited them from my late father, who would be guiding me in filling the application form from above, my guardian angel.

Nationality, I never know what to write, Nigerian or Black British, because I was born and grew up here, even though my parents are Nigerian. I have lived in East London for most of my life, but I did spend some memorable time in the late eighties in Nigeria, which was a real eye opener – but that's another story. I made some lifelong friends there and grew respect for my hard-working parents who came over here trying to make it.

Experience? What do I put down? Managing the students' behaviour was a requirement, I understood that I would not be teaching, just supervising classes, so it could not be that difficult, could it?

I have had a lot of experience in various fields that could relate to the classroom and managing students. Should I put down my experiences working in youth centres? One being Masbro Centre in Shepherd's Bush or Three Acres in Camden Town, where I would organise activities and trips for the children. I remember having so much fun myself, because I got to meet so many children from different backgrounds and abilities, seeing them interacting with each other and the staff. I would see the children's confidence grow in that short period of time and wonder how they would turn out as young adults.

Or should I put down that I was a Door Supervisor, otherwise known as a bouncer, for several years in the West End, then a Head Door woman, working with my own team at a busy, popular venue. I was a confident, energetic women and had won awards from my bosses for having excellent customer skills.

I even did an interview with the BBC on Women Door Supervisors in Central London with my dear friend Rachel, who was a 'too cool for school' kind of person and had way more experience than me.

She was a bad ass, doing close protection work for a lot of the bands at the time. She was known and respected by a majority of the venues in the West End and taught me how to handle myself on the door as a woman. Working together we had the best time, we could always deescalate a situation without violence and made sure our customers felt safe within the venues we worked at.

I read from the job description that the main role of a Cover Supervisor was to supervise the class, just like the name said, while the students were working on prepared work, ensuring that the students completed the work in the time given; this was to be done in an orderly and constructive way.

What about my current role as a Personal Assistant, with disabled clients? I thought this was an asset, as I could relay my experience that I gained in that field to any disabled students that I would have as students. "Yes I will put that down." It's a shame that there was not really any career development in that field because I really enjoyed it, and that's why I had started looking for other work, so that I could progress and have some kind of career and be able to provide for my nephew, Seun.

He was at an age now, where I could work longer hours, as I did not need to walk with him to and from school, he was gaining his confidence and wanted to go by himself or with his school friends. He was an intelligent strong-willed boy and at a stage where he loved school, gaining new friends and trying to sort everyone else's problems out, sometimes at his own cost. At least I knew, if anything happened to him, I would be able to get there quickly if I got the job at Rokeby, as it was nearby, it would be a new beginning, providing a better life for him.

Qualifications? Educated to GCSE Maths and English, I got that, plus A levels and a degree in Mechanical Engineering, that should be sufficient for this scale 5 post, I said to myself.

Many people asked, why I did not follow a career in Engineering. When my father passed away, I had to support the household financially, back when I was living with my mother. I did not have the luxury of looking for engineering work, which at the time was mostly in Europe. Should I have left my widowed mother and disabled brother? Bills had to be paid and life goes on. I feel all the better for it, because I have been lucky to meet some fantastic people on my life's journey, that I would not have encountered, if I had followed a different path, and that has made me who I am as a person today.

If I was finding the role hard, I am sure I will receive the necessary training." I can do this!" I muttered to myself and proceeded to fill out the application form, trying to put in all my relevant experience according to the person specification. I checked and double checked for mistakes. Fingers crossed, I whispered to myself and mailed it off.

A large envelope from the school came approximately a few weeks later.

"Should I open it now, or sit down?" I thought nervously, as my heart pounded in my chest.

"Why am I so worked up?" I asked myself, screw the suspense; I ripped it open, brought the bunch of papers out, and scanned the top sheet.

SATURDAY JUNE 6TH, 2020

We are pleased to inform you that you have been shortlisted and have been invited for an interview...

I was so happy, what great news! I continued to read on; part of the interview was me having to teach a Maths lesson to a Year 8 class. My heart sank, I thought, how will I keep the students' attention? How should I approach the topic of shapes with them? How do I start the lesson? Will they listen to me? What resources do I need?

I rang up to confirm my attendance, and got on with preparing myself for the interview. Over the next few days, I got a lesson plan in place, which involved a mini competition, identifying shapes, and a practical. Which, I am sure the students would enjoy, making 3D shapes with match sticks and blu-tack.

The school was 10 minutes' walk from Stratford station, just beyond the Broadway, which was convenient, because I lived in Stratford and knew a lot of the local youth. London had just won the 2012 Olympics and Newham was going to be home for the Olympic village. A shopping centre was going to be built called Westfield, apparently the biggest in Europe; there was a buzz around town.

As I walked along Stratford high road on the interview day, my dark skin glowed from the cocoa butter I had thoroughly greased my skin with from head to toe (could not have any dry patches on such an important day). I glanced at my refection in the local sweet shop window. I looked rather smart. At 5ft 9, some people might describe me as stocky at size 20/22, but I would always say curvy – *'must have some meat on the bones'* my dad would always say. I had on my lucky Black Doc Martens shoes, so I would be comfortable as I moved around the classroom during the lesson. I had on black trousers and a dark shirt, with my black shoulder length braids tied back in a pony-tail, the look was complete. I turned left onto Pitchford Street where the school was and hurried down as I wanted to be early for the interview.

The school was at the end of the road, with railings surrounding it. As you walked through the gates the car park was to the right. I was later to find out that the two-storey building on the left was the dining hall and directly in front of that, across the small yard was the science block, with classrooms leading off the long hallway. There was a mature tree, just by the science building, with its branches overlooking a bench, which I could imagine students sitting on and enjoying lunch.

I continued forward onto the reception, and saw the other four candidates. We were all admiring the display on the walls that the students had done. After making small talk among ourselves, we were all taken on a tour individually by two smartly dressed boys around the school at different times during the day. I remember thinking this is a lot to take in. First the staff room, walking straight through to the library, which had windows looking out to the front of the school. Followed by the Maths department, which was on two floors. Then up the stairs to the next two floors to the English department, then back down to the ground floor, past reception, admin staff, Deputy heads and the Head teacher's offices, through to the back of the science block and back out to the mature tree via the long hall.

We then walked around the English/Maths block, passing the gym, otherwise known as the PE department, which the boys were eager to point out. We then headed towards the massive playground, with a football pitch on one side; the external unit building for excluded students with an office and classrooms were next to the edge of the pitch. Next to that was the Pastoral building, which housed the RE department, some offices and a space with a sink and comfy chairs, which I imagined the students used for meetings or clubs.

Walking along the side of the Pastoral Building, we walked through double doors, with the Drama department to our left and the computer assistance office to our right. We then went upstairs leading to the Students with Educational Needs and Citizenship/

Humanities departments and that led us to the back of the staffroom. We continued forward through another set of double doors and back downstairs to a courtyard, otherwise known as the Art department, with various classrooms used for specific lessons: Art, Computer, Design and Technology, Cookery and Graphics lessons.

We then backtracked our steps out to the first double doors, where the music room was pointed out to us to the right, but we went straight ahead through a single door, which brought us out into the assembly hall. It was an impressive sight with polished floors. It had a high ceiling and a stage with curtains. The walls were covered with amazing, colourful artwork, chairs stacked up at the back and two or three sets of double doors to let the students in and out, I would imagine relatively quickly. We went through one of the double doors and as if by magic, we were back in reception.

At this stage, I was happy to have been wearing my Doc Martens, as I could see one of the other candidates grimacing with discomfort; she quickly took the opportunity to sit down. I gave her a look and smiled, to say, "I feel your pain, we have truly done our quota of exercise for the day!"

My interview was led by Grant Leppard with Seamus Fox chipping in with a few questions now and then. Seamus was Irish and reminded me of someone who had had a full life, but was still only halfway there. He was quite laid back, instantly likeable, white, tall and quite slender, slight shadow of a beard and short, kind of wavy dark hair. Grant was white, shorter, with a slight beer belly and brown short hair, greying at the sides. The most memorable discussion during the interview were about my experiences as a Door Supervisor and how I had coped being a woman. I could see they found it intriguing, questions like "How did you deal with rowdy clientele, in a male-dominated environment? How did you handle yourself?"

"Women deal with those situations better, as egos are not normally an issue," I replied, pleasantly recalling those days.

I remember one of them saying the lesson I was to teach was just to see whether I could manage a class full of students, and I should not worry too much about the quality of my teaching. I said I was happy that it was a Maths lesson, as I enjoyed Maths because it was a universal subject and crossed any barriers.

The lesson itself could not have gone any better, the students were all well behaved. Naively I thought it had something to do with my teaching, but looking back now, I think the good behaviour and engagement of the students had something to do with them having their normal teacher present, plus the person observing me; also the class was a top set. I felt quietly confident that I had got the role as I left the school that day.

A few days later, I received a small envelope. I knew it was from the school.

"This is not good, the envelope is too thin," I thought to myself as I felt it and frowned. I already knew its contents before I opened it, but I had to open it to confirm. Inside was a letter simply stating:

Unfortunately, you have not been given the role. That was the only line I saw.

"The calibre of the other applicants must have been really high, how disappointing!" I muttered to myself and I might have said a swear word or two.

Even though I was dis-heartened that I was not one of the chosen two, time flew by. A few months later, as preparations for Christmas were underway, with the frenzy of anticipation gripping the nation, I received a phone call from Grant Leppard out of the blue. After the initial pleasantries, he said to my amazement:

Grant: Are you still available for the Cover Supervisor role?

Me: Yes of course, when do you want me to start? (I said without even thinking about it.)

Grant: After the Christmas holidays, we have staff training on the first day back.

Me: Great, I'll see you then!

He then went on to tell me, exactly what date, and roughly what I would be doing in the first week. I held on to the phone tightly, not wanting to miss a single piece of information, answering with quick "Hmms, Yes, ok" at the appropriate intervals, even though in my mind I was buzzing. Why did they choose me? Am I ready for this, what do I have to rearrange to take on this opportunity? Ultimately, I was chuffed and could not wait to embrace this new challenge. I was so happy to get a chance to work in an academic environment, actually working with students, watching them learn, I simply could not wait to start!

January 2007

With a spring to my step, filled with aspiration and enthusiasm, I made my way to the school on the 3rd of January 2007. It was a training day for all the staff: teachers, administrative staff, personal assistants, technicians, teaching assistants, everyone was there.

There were large tables laid out in the assembly hall with paperwork and resources piled on top to complete tasks during the sessions, chairs were dotted around the tables, it was quite overwhelming. There must have been close to hundred people there, I remember thinking, how am I going to remember everyone's names? Which departments did they all work in?

The table I sat at had approximately ten people. The day consisted of plans for the term and brainstorming ideas in our groups, on what we would do to publicise and market the school. One of the men on my table who was quite friendly was Fulbert. He told me he was a French teacher and Head of Year 10. He was wearing an African print top, he looked like a chief of an African tribe, over 6ft and of dark complexion; you could see he was a bit of a lady charmer and a chatterer. Next, we were all given a folder and directed to look at the exam results and discuss the priorities for the year ahead. I was so engrossed in all of it, soaking in all the information given.

Charlotte Robinson was the head teacher; she welcomed everyone back from the festive season and introduced the new staff. She was about 5ft 5 with heels, slender and well endowed, her brown hair was cut to frame her face, she spoke with authority and you could see she was energised and ready for the new term. I later found out that she was a Maths teacher, who worked with the students predicted A* and A's in their GCSE exams.

"Wow!" I thought, how inspirational!

A few of the staff went outside during a break, and I followed and introduced myself. Everyone was chatting and exchanging Christmas stories, saying who had travelled where and wishing the holiday had gone on for longer. Fulbert and a woman named Ina Joshua were closest to me, Ina was a Higher Learner Teacher Assistant (HLTA), which is the next level to a Teaching Assistant (TA); she was talking about her daughter and teenagers' issues. She was a chatty one too, about 5ft, wearing jeans and a hijab so her head was covered. She would ask a question, but before you could finish replying, another one would be asked. I smiled, her enthusiasm was infectious as I listened to her tales.

I was told that I was replacing a lady called Bethany, who had left suddenly in the previous term. There was speculation on her reasons for leaving, but it went over my head, as I did not know who or what they were referring to. Ina had worked in the school for several years and said she hated the term after Christmas because the students took too long to settle into a routine after the excessive food and late nights.

During the day, I got chatting to a lady called Debbie Ward. She was a Behaviour/Learning Mentor and had a radiance of self-confidence about her. During lunch, she commented about the food needing some more spice, and I thought to myself:

"Me and her are going to get on just fine!"

I would later find out that she did so much more within the school, but was not recognised for it. I think her motives were just for the boys and she wanted the best for them, she herself had only started working at the school in the previous autumn term.

I found out that she was Caribbean heritage from St Kitts, was born and grew up in Bradford. With her long wavy, black hair that she normally packed in a tight neat bun at the back of her head, you would be forgiven if you mistook her as mixed race. Debbie had a slender figure and was roughly my height; I would have placed her at late twenties, but I later found out she was much older than that.

The rest of the day went well, getting to know the staff, I felt as if I fitted in. I looked around at some point during the day as everyone was talking among themselves and was contented to be part of this team and my enthusiasm blossomed for what could be possible in the future.

Anyway, I was soon introduced to Tony Green, who gave me a timetable of classes I was to observe over the next few days. I was to observe how the teachers interacted with the students and pick up tips I could use myself. Tony was pleasant enough with an East end accent. He was young, about 22, with a lot of energy, quite short, with filled out pink cheeks and short, black spikey hair. I never really knew his job title, but he was part of the English department and taught a few of the bottom set classes or students on reduced timetable. Even though he was not a teacher, he had his way with the boys and they were quite fond and responded well to him. His direct line manager was Mick Eyres, whom I was to report to if I had any problems.

Tony was my immediate manager, but as nice as he was, he didn't really have a clue on how to advise me on certain issues, because he did not have hardly any experiences either, so he would always direct me to Mick.

Mick was always busy. If I wanted to know something that I could not find out myself, I would walk and talk with him, because he was always rushing somewhere or another, so you had to get the information on the go.

After a day or two, I was left to get on with it. In the mornings my cover slip for the day would be in my pigeonhole between 8.00-8.30am, then I would rush around the various departments to see whether work had been left. Failing that I would go to the Heads of Department and if that didn't work, find something out of my resources box that I had started to put together.

The person who arranged cover was a lady called Wendy, she was the one you would get at the other end of the phone, when you called in sick. She was like a school matron, and she would often boast that she had never had an emergency sick day and did not understand why anyone would want a day off. Wendy was also religious when it came to her lunch – you could set your watch by her, because she was always on time for it!

For the three years I was there, I could count how many times I saw her smile. She was tall and stocky, similar to my build, but thinner, and she would wear short skirts and heels, quite an imposing figure, when walking towards you; with her severe cut bob, she portrayed the image of being confident and self-reliant.

I can understand why she had that attitude. Having to organise the cover rota for the whole school, using teachers, agency workers and the cover supervisor to cover all the classes in all the departments was not an easy task. She started to take calls from 7.30am and most probably would have to change the rota several times before 8.30am – by then, you could tell she just wanted to pull the telephone cord out from the wall!

The school had been open since approximately 1965, it was for 11-16-year-old boys, who would enter in Year 7 and leave in Year 11. In the last 10 years, the school had started to gain a colourful reputation within the community, especially businesses in the shopping mall. The boys would hang out there during lunch and after school. I am sure it was only a minority that caused trouble, but those are the ones everyone remembers.

Newham in general was a deprived neighbourhood, with a high percentage of the students on free school meals. Even though a lot of the parents wanted the best for their children, it was not easy for them to put food and a roof over the children's head and at the same time, be there for them after school and supervise them. I am sure in an ideal world they would have jumped at the chance to have that opportunity to stay at home and just raise their kids without any financial worry, but that choice was not available.

The school had a high percentage of students from ethnic minorities; African, Caribbean, Asian and even Eastern European within the school. It was beautiful watching all these cultures mix and hearing the different languages being spoken during break times.

The role of a Cover Supervisor was to cover lessons from all subjects when the main teacher was absent; you needed to be able to think on your feet and adapt the work accordingly, but most of all, you had to be really on top of your behaviour management. I was able to give praise and sanctions all in one breath, but the boys knew importantly that I was fair and consistent and they liked that.

I was surprised that I was expected to cover classes in all of the departments, but I thought, maybe this is a good way to learn the ropes, and get to know the students. Hopefully, I would be assigned to fewer departments after a while, fingers crossed.

The first few classes were a learning curve. The students were intrigued to see a new member of staff, and tried to push my buttons, by saying things like: "You are not our teacher, so we are not doing the work!"

"We have not done this before, we don't know what to do!"

"Our teacher normally lets us watch You-tube videos!"

"We don't know where our books are, so we can't work!"

"Miss, I left my pen at home, so I can't write…"

"We do not understand the work, so we cannot do it."

I managed to avert all the distractions and get them to complete the work given, I had watched various staff and picked up tips on how to handle the students quickly. I could have listened to all their complaints and given in, but their teachers were expecting work to be completed and I had to establish myself as a credible member of staff, otherwise I knew the students would walk all over me, if given a chance.

I took to the job like a duck to water. I was so confident and you could clearly see I was enjoying the job. No subject was out of bounds, apart from PE! Thank God I never had to cover apart from the odd occasion. I would have to hold the changing room door with one hand and with the other hand covering my nose, trying to ignore the intense smell wafting in my direction and yell for all of them to get out…all part of being a team player, I suppose!

Coming from working in security, I was able to project my voice to the back of the queue to give essential information to the club customers: "We are not letting anyone in that's wearing trainers" or "it's one in and one out" and the best one "Make your way out, please!". Using this skill in the classroom was very useful as it enabled me to get a student's attention, without having to shout. The students hated me standing next to them, when I was talking; they would say my voice was too loud!

I would try and pack up: collect books and pile them in the correct location and keep the classroom tidy for the next lesson, picking up any rubbish off the floor before leaving. I would write a brief summary of the outcome of the lesson, five minutes before the end, so as the bell went, I was ready to let the students out, lock the door and make the dash to the next lesson. I would sigh with relief, if I got my cover slip, and I was covering for one or two teachers or a double lesson for the day, because it would mean, I would not have to be dashing around the school when the bell went.

One of the many useful pieces of information that Debbie pointed out to me at the start was to familiarize myself with each room and where things were kept, so I would not be in a panic, when the students were present. The advantage of being a real teacher is having your own classroom, as you know where things are and are already in your classroom for the day, calmly awaiting your next class.

Depending on how many staff were absent, I would do four to five lessons a day, plus my duties. It was always busy, and even though I had no previous experience of working in a classroom, I improvised and got on with it.

This was appreciated and I got a lot of positive feedback from the teachers and other members of staff too and that raised my confidence and job satisfaction even further.

My fashion style was dark casual attire, joggers and sweatshirts as I wanted to be comfortable while moving around the school. One of the things that the students liked about me was the different trainers I wore. I would get comments like:

"Oh Miss, your trainers look buff!"

Another student: "Where did you buy them from?"

I heard one student talking to another student while pointing at my feet. "I bet she gets hooked up with a discount, maybe she knows someone who works there?" I think they felt they could relate to me through my trainers.

Back in the day, when I was a child, you would be extremely brave to ask your teachers about their sexuality, but nowadays the kids just bluntly come out with it,

"Ms Sandy, are you married?" as they would look at my ring. I would hesitate before answering, because I knew it would lead to more questions.

"Yes", then I would hear:

"No way, she looks gay, maybe she is married to a woman!"

"Miss, are you gay?"

"Does it matter?" I would reply, never confirming or denying their questions, waiting for them to dare say something, let them strew on that. I wanted them to embrace whoever was teaching them, regardless who that person has chosen to be with.

***

One of the memorable events from the early days, was when I had run out of space on the normal white board, and had one more task for the students that needed to be completed for that lesson. I proceeded to write on the interactive white board with a blue marker pen, thinking it was just a normal board. One of the boys, saw what I was doing and shrieked loudly with laughter:

"Look, Miss is writing on the interactive white board!" he said in amazement.

All the boys looked up, and someone said, "You won't be able to wipe it off"; another one said, "Miss has spoiled our teacher's board!"

More laughter and signs of exclamations from the class.

Another student said in a low voice, but loud enough for me to hear, "How could she be so stupid to write on the interactive white board!"

I just stood there, while the students were commenting, horrified at what I had done. I proceeded to try and wipe the board with a damp duster.

Someone sniggered, "As if that's gonna work!"

I turned around and said in a calm voice, "Nothing to worry about, guys, I'm sure it can be cleaned," not really believing myself when I said it, but praying.

"Those boards are really expensive to replace and you used a permanent marker, Miss," a student said with oversized glasses, perched on the tip of his nose.

I replied sarcastically, "Thank you for letting me know, I am sure it won't get to that."

"Shut the hell up!" is really what I wanted to say to him, but I used all of my willpower to resist.

I wished the ground could just swallow me up right there and then and whisk me to a poolside on a sunny day, sipping on a Pina colada cocktail, anywhere but right here and right now.

I quickly said, taking a deep breath, "Ok, class, start to pack up, and pass your exercise books to the front!" All the students were talking about was the white board among themselves as they filed out of the room, rushing to go for their break.

Thank heavens, it was break next so I dashed out too, looking for the caretaker, Les. I called him the 'saviour', because no job was too big for him. He was a tall, skinny man, late forties (I think), with a heart of gold and quite fit – he runs marathons for charity and walked everywhere!

"Don't panic, Shola," he said, "I have got something for that." He dropped everything he was doing and followed me back to the classroom.

Using the special fluid on a cloth, he was able to slowly remove the offending blue marks.

I sighed with relief that my first month's salary was not going to go on replacing a white board; needless to say, I have never made that mistake again.

"Thanks, Les, you are an absolute life saver!"

Sunday June 7th, 2020

I watched in amazement when I saw on the news the topping of the Edward Colston statue, the slave trader in Bristol, by the Black Lives Matters protesters. I remember noting the colours of the hands holding the straps, pulling down the statue were mainly white, it was like the '*United Colours of Benetton*'. I was reassured that we were not in the battle alone, there were crowds all around, cheering them along, with handwritten banners. Phones were in the air waiting for the unforgettable moment. It started to lean and with a final tug it was down; as it fell the crowds jeered loudly with fists up in the air.

Red paint was poured on him, an afro comb was placed on his head and a juice carton of something or other from Jamaica was placed on him, absolutely hilarious! And to solidify the moment, various people took turns to stand on him and take selfies! Priceless!

Then to top it off, the protesters tied a rope to the top and bottom of the remaining statue. Working in a team, some leading the way, some pulling with the ropes, some physically rolling it down the road, all around being cheered and supported by swarms of people of all nationalities. When they finally reached the harbour edge, they manged to manoeuvre the metal carcass over the metal barrier and into the harbour, plonk! Wow! It was like watching a movie; the police watched it happen and said later that intervening would have caused more drama.

In my opinion it was such a wonderful sight, just as he had trafficked over 80,000 slaves from Africa to the West Indies and

America in those boats, chained in inhumane conditions, a lot of them did not survive the journey. Some chose the option of jumping into the sea to their deaths as that was a better option to the rape, starvation, abuse and torture they were going through on the boat, not to mention the fact that they were torn from their families and the land that they knew and loved.

"My ancestors that you forced from their land had no choice, but to go in the sea, so now you have some of that, you fucker!" as I pointed and jeered at the TV.

I learnt afterwards that there had been a petition for years with such huge support to remove his statue, but to no avail. With the momentum of the last few weeks, it felt like this was the time, permission given or not!

"That monstrosity must come down now!"

The town of Bristol was built with much of his wealth, roads and buildings were named after him, portraits of him were even hung in City Hall. The city has come a long way from 1963 – back then the bus companies refused to employ black people; thankfully the Bristol black citizens boycotted the buses, which led to the *'Race Relations Act'* making it illegal to discriminate.

Soon after the toppling, key institutions that held his name started to have the conversation and even some were brave enough to drop his name.

I heard that the remains were dragged out of the harbour and stored in a secret location, to be placed in a museum, hopefully with the complete historical information about him for future generations to be informed correctly.

***

In London there were protests too, but it seemed with heightened energy this time. People were hanging from traffic lights; signs were placed on various statues. The Churchill statue had been vandalised with placards and graffiti *"Churchill was a racist"* was scribbled on his pith. Far right protesters were present too and they were not impressed with the disrespect of Churchill's statue.

***

Meanwhile in Oxford, Cecil Rhodes' statue on the face of Oriel College was too high for protesters to reach, but that didn't stop them from gathering below with their banners, chanting:

"Take it down take it down!"

I remember watching the news and seeing the view from above – police climbers were on the roof to protect anyone from reaching him. I did not know much about him – I had to go and look him up. Apparently, he was a diamond miner and had a scholarship named after him.

***

There has been a lot of conversation regarding confederate flags in America. My personal feelings about it are not positive – the flag signifies to me times of oppression of my people and I have observed that right wing protesters always seem to have it flying away with pride from their houses and cars. I didn't understand why it was still being displayed with pride on some public buildings in America in 2020. What did it truly represent for some people, I wonder?

Reading up on the confederate flags, it was used by the Confederate States Army during the US Civil War. Those bastards were fighting against the United State forces so they could uphold white supremacy and the institution of slavery in the Southern states of America. Can you imagine?

SUNDAY JUNE 7TH, 2020

In a statement released on the 6th of June by The US Marines Corps, they ordered the removal of confederate flags in public spaces on its military bases and work areas including offices buildings. Our ancestors would be clapping and celebrating in their graves at the news, as that flag, that image must have sparked up real fear within them with the possibility of death back then during those awful times.

***

Back to school…

Initially, I just made it up as I went along, finding out what worked and what didn't. What was crucial was knowing each and every name of all the boys in the school and trying to pronounce it right. It's amazing the positive response I got when I took the time to do that, because each child felt important and after a while I got to know their individual personalities.

Mick Eyres taught Maths, among other managerial roles within the school, and one of those roles was being in charge of any newly qualified teachers, when they started working at the school.

I observed him teaching a few of his lessons; he was so organised and obviously enjoyed teaching the subject. His classroom was based in the Pastoral building, opposite his office. He walked with a slight arrogance around the school, I put it down to the fact that he had worked there for several years and he knew his stuff inside out.

Mick was an interesting man to talk to, because he was so different to me, going to the right schools and mixing with the right people with similar backgrounds. Living somewhere in Essex, by the sea, he would commute into Stratford on the train and bike the rest of the way; even though he had a previous back injury, he still liked to keep fit. He said it was the years of playing rugby, that made him enjoy keeping fit; over 6ft, he was stocky, with wide shoulders, a head full of black, slightly grey short hair, the tan he had seemed permanent, as if he had a bit of Mediterranean in him, I later found out, it was just because he was an outside person.

The teachers made it all look so easy including Mick, and it would be many years, before I understood what it really took to get them to that stage of confidence. Debbie was extremely helpful, identifying staff by their names and most importantly, giving me an insight to the boys' lives. Looking back now, I do not know what I would have done without her support.

Ina Joshua was equally helpful, showing me shortcuts to get from A to B, how and where to get computer access and photocopy log in details. Also, where to get a fob for the main gate and keys to access all the classrooms and staff toilets. It was a lot of keys to carry around, as I was in so many classrooms.

Lunch duty

On top of doing the cover work, I was required to do lunch duty every day; I thought it would be a good idea to get to know the students outside of the classroom, even if it meant I didn't have lunch myself. The lunch time period was like a military operation, which is understandable, as it's a difficult task getting 900 rowdy, hungry boys to collect their food, eat and leave ready for period 5 in 45 minutes.

The students queued up outside in their year groups. A member of the Senior Leadership Team (SLT) would be at the door, then they would be let in, in batches depending on their conduct. They would then have to queue again at the bottom of the stairs that led to the food hall. The SLT comprised teachers who had departmental responsibility or were line managers, because of this they did not have a full teaching rota, so had time to carry out other roles like the one above.

Ms Robinson would be standing on the second or third step and would then inspect the uniforms of the students before letting them up. Two dinner monitors were at the top of the stairs with staff from the admin department, checking names against the register and giving a token if they were on free school meals. The monitors would than signal Ms Robinson when to send more students up the stairs, keeping a constant flow, till everyone was up. There were separate stairs on the other side of the hall leading downstairs and out of the building, so in practice everything should run smoothly and everyone should be fed with no issues.

The dinner monitors had to be in Year 10 or 11 and apply for the post, as if applying for a job; this was good experience in my opinion and taught the boys a lot of skills, which could be put on their CV. There were about eight or more monitors placed in strategic places around the dining hall, all having specific roles and were rotated around periodically.

Once up the stairs and in the hall, the students would then have to queue, forming a line, against a wall, separated by a slight barrier from the rest of the dining hall to collect a tray. The hall was quite big with high ceilings and large windows, which did not open for obvious reasons, like food being used as missiles from the top floor to unsuspecting students below. There were large rectangle tables with attached seating spaced out, leaving room to walk in-between; cold food was served at one end of the counter and the other end was hot food. During the summer it would be extremely hot in there, especially when everyone was inside, so it was important to keep the atmosphere calm and constantly flowing.

I would get there as quickly as I could after my lesson just as the operation was getting started, I would always make a point of addressing Charlotte, as "Ms Robinson", when I said hello to her passing her on the way up the stairs, in front of the students, as I thought it was important to show respect to the Head teacher, model appropriate behaviour as they say.

Once in the dining hall, I would always say hi to Denise, who was the head cook, and the one who collected the token or money, just before you got your food. Denise was a feisty one; she could give as good as she got from the boys and had overall responsibility for the kitchen staff.

My duties were to position myself at the end of the food line, making sure that the students were behaving in an orderly fashion; also:

Ensuring the lunch monitors were in their allocated places.

Making sure the boys having school dinners took their trays and emptied them properly.

To resolve any problems that arose, making sure that the pupils vacated the dining hall in time for fifth period.

To take items of lost property to reception and to report any incidences that occurred in the hall.

I was very serious with my responsibility, handling it like a military mission.

I was lucky to have Debbie doing lunch duty with me and one member of SLT floating in the hall, while others sat down having their lunch. Once all students were in from the outside, Ms Robinson would then come up, walk around and then leave the hall going past me.

Once she left, the remaining SLT members would leave, muttering some excuse or another, and it would be just Debbie and I that would hurry the remaining students along and get them out before the next lesson. Denise and her crew started to clean up the hall by then, around 1.35pm, because they had to leave soon after.

The first time I did this duty, I felt overwhelmed. I can't describe the feeling of trying to control hungry boys that could smell food and see their peers eating, but had to wait in a queue. I remember saying in a sarcastic voice, "Stop behaving as if you are in market!", in response to them pushing, shoving and trying to jump the queue by intimidating the younger ones. It was always worse, when it was raining or towards the end of term.

One memorable incident that happened in the dining hall during the early part of my time at Rokeby was when a few Year 10 students were mimicking some younger students sitting at a table close to the queuing line. One comment, said too much by the elder student, led to the younger one flying from his table to hit the Year 10 student; the older boy dodged the attempt and grabbed the younger boy, using his collar as a lever to propel himself over the barrier. Before you could blink, more students had come from either side, just for the hell of it and there was a massive pile up, with punches and food flying everywhere; it was like a scene out of a movie, without anyone to say "Cut!". Debbie and I flew over, plus any members of staff that were eating in the hall at the time.

We managed to separate the culprits, but the damage was done, torn uniforms, blood streaming down one of the boys' faces mixed with sweat, and each one panting, blaming the other, the dining hall was a mess, and the military operation sabotaged. I remember thinking that happened in a second; from that moment on, Debbie and I were always extra attentive in the hall.

But leaving the dining hall through the back stairs was another matter. I hated holding on to the banister when going down the stairs because nine times out of ten, the students would have put ketchup or mayonnaise on the banister or some other sauce. I got caught out once, rushing down the stairs trying to get to my lesson on time, wondering why the banister was so wet, looking down and seeing my hand dripping with brown sauce, absolutely disgusting (considering it was not my choice of sauce) but still, anyway never again! Despite all my investigations, I never found the damn rascals responsible for this regular nasty occurrence!

Wages

My first wages I thought were off and I had still not received my contract, so I spoke to Grant. He didn't know anything about it, so he told me to go to Shelley, the school administrator. She was in her office trying to look busy. She briskly told me to wait for my contract, and I thought, 'Well, I am sure they will reimburse me my proper wages, once my contract arrives', and didn't think too much more about it.

I never managed to chit chat with Shelley – some people are just not suited for that. She was strictly business with me, which was good enough for me and she always looked busy, so I only spoke to her when needed.

Her appearance was very childlike, even though she must have been in her late thirties. I could never quite place my finger on it, maybe it was that she was quite petite and flat chested or that she wore dresses revealing too much flesh, wearing chunky, ill-fitted high heels, or was it just her timid speech? Shelley had shoulder length dark hair and looked Mediterranean, she was one of those people who never seemed to have a genuine smile, and I could never figure out why.

***

When my contact finally arrived weeks later, I had to blink when I saw my salary, and blink again; I brought the paper up close, and read the information again.

£13,000 approximately! "There must be some mistake!" I said to myself.

I scanned down though the rest of the contract, and on page 2, it mentioned the need to attend a Teaching Assistant training course. Once completed you would be placed on scale 5 and moved up that scale incrementally, until you reached the upper limit.

The next day, as soon as I could, I went to Shelley's office. I refused to leave until she saw me or made a time for me to return. Reluctantly,

SUNDAY JUNE 7TH, 2020

she said she could briefly see me now.

I said, "There seems to be some misunderstanding, with my salary, Shelley," at the same time passing the contact to her.

"I have been placed on scale 4, I don't understand," I continued.

Even without looking at it, she said, "Yes, you have been placed on scale 4, because you have not completed the Teaching Assistant course yet; once you complete the course you will be moved onto scale 5."

I contemplated this for a moment, and said, "What course? I was not told of this before, this is a huge difference to what I was expecting, am I really on scale 4? Is there nothing you can do?"

She looked at the contract." Well, I will look into it, and get back to you." She handed the contract back to me and looked down, as if getting on with her work, obviously my cue to leave. As expected, she always said the minimum amount of words to me. I said thank you and left the matter in her hands, worried that I would not be able to meet all my financial requirements.

***

I received another contract soon after the first one, I immediately turned to page 2, and this time it was approximately £16,000. I took it to Shelley again.

"It's great my wages have increased, any ideas why it's still short? I am getting concerned as it's lower than the advert advertised."

Then she said that she had moved me to the top of scale 4 and when I completed the TA course, she said, I would be moved on to scale 5 and "your wages will be backdated".

"Really?"

I asked her how soon I could go on the course; she replied that it was best to speak to my line manager.

***

I promptly went back to Grant.

"Shelley says I need to attend a course for my wages to be right, do you know anything about it?"

"I am not sure, maybe ask Daniel about it and what wages he gets."

To be honest I didn't feel comfortable asking someone else about their wages – who does that in a professional setting? I did summon the guts to ask Daniel in the end, and he was quite free with the information; he said he was on the top of scale 4. He confirmed he would be getting his wages backdated once he finished the course later in the year. I felt reassured, but still worried as he was put on the training as soon as he started working at the school and I was still waiting.

***

At the next meeting I raised this issue about this apparent training with Mick, Tony and even Grant. I was told I would be starting next term, which I presumed was September of that year. I was not thrilled with this, as I thought it was important to have the relevant training right away for the job I was already doing. Secondly, I was going to be out of pocket financially until I had completed the course, and there was nothing I could do to change this fact.

***

Daniel Hayes aka Lazy or L was the other Cover Supervisor. He was a tall, slender man and a single father to a young daughter. I wanted to support him as I felt he was doing the best under the circumstances; he covered mostly PE and English and I seemed to be down for the rest of the subjects.

At first, I didn't catch on that Lazy was really that lazy. I just thought he needed a hand now and then, but when you put it all together, he was taking the mick out of me. I didn't realise until a while later.

> **L:** Oh Shola, I see you have a free period, could you cover my lesson for me?
>
> **Me**: Sure thing, L!

Another day

> **L**: Oh Shola, could you do my break duty?
>
> **Me**: No problem, L!
>
> **L:** I need to leave for a meeting, can you cover the last 15 mins of my lesson?
>
> **Me:** Will be right there, L!

Also, he was on this training course and I wanted him to do well, so I picked up all the slack for the remainder of that academic year. I never ever asked him to help me out in any way; maybe I should have been a bit needy and not so efficient, looking back now.

Connexions

We had a gentleman called Chris Jarvis from Connexions, a service that provided advice to teenagers among other services. He was our Careers Adviser and was supposed to come into the school once a week; he was based in the Pastoral Centre. Mick asked me to assist Chris with his workload. This had been agreed at an SLT meeting; I didn't really have a choice in the matter, so I ended up working a lot with Chris and intervening with those hard to reach students, especially when he could not make it during the school day.

I made sure we had all the brochures for all the Sixth forms, colleges and a lot of universities laid out in order, posters up on the walls about various courses, apprenticeships, open days and any work opportunities. The students would come to me and ask for advice or information. I really enjoyed helping and assisting them in mapping out a plan for their future.

September 2007

It was a new term, and having done two, I felt I was getting better at my job, because of the compliments I received from the teachers and the relationship I was building with the students. I had by then built up a collection of resources in my stash bag. If class work was not left by the teacher, I had something to fall back on, if only for ten minutes, while I looked frantically for relevant work. For example, I had specific subject word-searches, pre-printed subject worksheets, and a lot of logical and mental tasks for the students to be getting on with.

I would also liaise with the '*Special Educational Needs*' department (SEN) to get advice on specific students. This was helpful, as it gave me background on the student, for example if a student had ADHD, they would give me strategies to assist with keeping that particular student engaged.

I had a few teachers that I admired and they mostly seemed to be in the Maths department. One of them was Brian Tobin, who had something about him the students loved. I observed him teaching and tried to put my finger on it. I think it was the fact that he had a sense of humour and had real banter with the students. The lesson was always fast-paced, with him firing quick questions and the students replied with equal vigour; the students loved it, and an hour always

SUNDAY JUNE 7TH, 2020

seemed to fly by. When I asked him later, he said he could relate to the boys and it seemed they could relate to him too. He made them enjoy Maths, which can be quite hard to do.

Another teacher was Jo Walker, now she was so organised and I knew if I was covering her lesson, I would not have to worry. She had a seating plan with names, detailed work and all the resources I needed, plus extra work in case anyone finished. She also informed the class and told them what she expected to hear on her return. I enjoyed covering her lessons, because I knew the students were learning and well behaved. No one messed with Jo – I think it's because she was fair and would always follow though, with what she said. I picked up tips from both of them and tried to apply it to my lessons.

I had attended a one-day course in the previous term called '*You are not a real teacher*'; it was aimed at Cover Supervisors. I literally begged to attend the course, just to know whether I was doing the right thing. It was great to go on some personalized training, it was very useful, but not much training can be done in a day.

What I really wanted to do was the Teaching Assistant course. Daniel had completed the course in the June/July and he said to me on several occasions that his pay was going to be backdated from when he started in September 2006.

I thought to myself, "I will be in the same position as him this time next year, with a nice tidy sum of back pay, so I will be able to finally repair my windows at home and get something nice for my gorgeous nephew, Seun," who was living with me at the time.

September came and went…

I was expecting to be told details about the course and when I was starting, but no one said anything to me about it. I kept on asking Mick, Grant and even Tony what was going on with the course, but to no avail. Daniel aka Lazy had said he had been put on the course automatically and didn't understand why it was not the same for me. Finally, Mick said I could not go on the course this year, word from senior management, he was not clear on the reason, and he would not volunteer any further information. I was deeply upset by this change in position and just did not understand why; I had worked extremely hard and felt as though I had just been fobbed off, especially as they said I would be able to do the course once Daniel had finished. I was told that definitely next year I would be put on the course; I should just be patient.

Meanwhile, the Career Advising that Mick wanted me to do for the Year 11s, was much more work than I ever imagined, on top of the three evenings a week, I would be in the Careers room in the Pastoral Centre on my own, doing much more than application forms. A lot of the boys did not even know what their plans were after school, so together we would find out what subjects they liked and their predicted grades, also what options were available. Chris would come into school once a week and conduct prearranged 20-minute one-to-one interviews with the students. This time was absolutely crucial, as it was the only professional career advice that the students were going to get. He would then send them a summary and advice on what to do next. He worked with other schools, so he was really overstretched, and that's why Mike thought it would be a good idea for me to support him and that was agreed with senior management.

One of the other tasks I did to make Chris's services more efficient, was to remind each student personally of their interview times with Chris. He visited mostly every Tuesday and even though the students were told of their appointment prior to the day, they had to be reminded because if for whatever reason they could not make it, someone else could be given that spot. I would rush around on Tuesday mornings to the different tutorial groups, firstly to make sure the students in question were in school, and secondly to give them a note to excuse them from class at the appointment time; this was in conjunction with doing my cover classes.

Furthermore, I would call up colleges and sixth forms and ask for their prospectus. I ordered boxes and boxes of them which were sent to the school; I would leave them in the Careers room and library for the students to pick up to pursue at their leisure. Also, any open day information and college fairs dates, I would place them strategically around the school, especially in the library and other main areas.

I tried to make the careers room more inviting and organised. Mick ordered colour-coded trays, with sticky labels to place the different college application forms in. Mick also wanted university prospectuses to enable the students who wanted to go to university to have a look at what was offered in the various institutions. As well as the above, any apprenticeship or training I was aware of would go up on the Pastoral board and I would help them fill out any application forms.

I helped with CVs, statements for work or educational establishments. The less Chris came in the more I did; even though it was not part of my job description, I did not want to let the students down.

"What do you want to do as a career in the future?" I would ask the students.

The most common answer I got was, "I want to be a footballer!"

"Nothing wrong with achieving your dreams," I would reply.

But when I showed them they would actually have to put in a lot of work into making that a reality: getting fit, watching their diet, training religiously and generally be highly disciplined and focused, you could see that some of the boys had not thought of the points I had raised.

"Nothing wrong with you having a plan B. Do you know how many professional footballers get injured and they don't have a plan B? So they end up broke with no qualifications. I don't want that to happen to you!"

We would then talk about other options, and I would let them know about the open days of local colleges to go and feel them out and ask further questions about a specific course that they may have been interested in.

Remember my hero Debbie? When I first started at that school, she was the one who showed me the ropes, where everything was; she did not have to do that, but I think she wanted to help a sister out and she could see I was passionate about the role. She looked like an African Queen and carried herself that way, she had an aura around her that drew people to her, including me.

In the mornings, she would walk around the local area to get the boys into the school before the bell went. Sometimes they would be in the corner shops, sometimes having a fag, sometimes just caught up chatting with their mates and had lost track of the time. I started doing it with her when I could; it was a good way to engage with the students to show we cared and to relate to them the importance of education and punctuality.

She would gather them up, those who had holes in their shoes, and she would go and buy them a new pair – she knew the families who could not afford it, so she did it discreetly. They were those who had no breakfast, so she would get them something to eat from the canteen, mostly with her own money.

Some came to school with dirty uniforms, that had the grease caked on the collar. She would pull them aside discreetly always, then look for clean clothes in lost property in their size or get something from the PE department, while they waited in her office. Then she would organise their uniform to be washed ready for the next school day. She just knew what to do for the student's well-being without being told.

We would stand by the gates and check uniforms and say to EVERY single student:

"Good morning!" with so much enthusiasm.

You would get funny looks or a couple of grunts from the students, or they would just put their heads down initially, embarrassed to engage with us.

But over time, we started to get positive replies. I think the boys appreciated it and it gave us time to have a quick chat with the students and see who was who.

"Morning, Miss!" they would say with a grin, walking into school.

"Morning, John, don't forget to pick up your school jumper from lost property," Debbie said to a boy who always had his head down and never replied.

"Oh yeah, thanks, Miss, have a good day, Miss" as he walked past us towards the main building.

Debbie and I looked at each other in shock and quickly replied, "You too, John!"

Debbie's role was a Behaviour/Learning Mentor, but she did so much more than that within the school; having raised two sons and a daughter and living in the area she had the skills to relate to these boys. They really respected and trusted her for what she did for them and how she always went the extra mile.

Black Pupil Achievement Programme (BPAP)

I was asked by Fulbert – remember the guy from my first day? I was on his table for the staff training – anyway he asked me to get involved in the BPAP. Which Mick thought was a good idea. At the time my involvement was going to meetings and supporting the selected students in revision classes and during the holidays, which I did. The project was born out of the fact that black boys were not reaching their full potential nationally, so money was available for incentives like this to improve the potential of the black boys in question, especially in deprived areas.

Sarah Lawson was the member of staff supposed to be running it. She spoke fluent French and was strongly in favour of equality. Although Sarah worked in the languages department, she also had other roles within the school, so was quite busy. She was a lovely person and her heart was in the right place, but as I said, she just did not have the time to do any justice to the project. Debbie was also involved and extremely motivated, so between the two of us and the support of a few staff, we undertook the task of expanding the remit of the BPAP and started to do after-school sessions and social events.

There was no pay for our work, just someone needed to take on the project and develop it out of love. We grasped it with both hands; this was exactly what the boys needed after school to keep them safe and focused. It was a time of heavy knife crime in London and our young black boys were killing or getting killed. Debbie and I were worried every day when the boys left the school, whether one of them would be next to be stabbed or worst-case scenario be the stabber, as the boys thought that by carrying a knife they were protecting themselves.

We were given a meagre allowance, which we added to, of course from our own pockets. It started slowly with just a handful of boys and steadily increased to over 30 or more boys. To cater for them we would buy bread, butter, ham, cheese, fruit, crisps and biscuits. They could also have a hot or cold drink. We bought another toaster and made full use of the kettle. We wanted the boys to concentrate on the tasks we were giving them to do, and for some of them, this was like a pre-dinner, something hot and heathy.

Debbie and I did so many activities with the boys: homework, career advice, how to engage with the police, relationships, financial stuff, moral issues, personal hygiene, debating and even learning how to sew a button on a shirt. We even bought an ironing board to make sure they knew how to iron properly and present themselves in the best light to the world.

Having the group helped me understand the boys more, I could keep an eye on their behaviour and academic progress, as I saw them in lessons and around the school. I had a lot of parents on speed dial on my phone and Debbie and I would try and intervene if an issue came up with the boys. They trusted us and confided in us, and through that we were able to prevent problems escalating.

One memorable highlight was organising a barbecue. The boys took control of buying, cooking, entertainment and clearing up. It was an amazing event and the boys learnt so many skills and how to appreciate each other even more.

Some of them really flourished, being selected to be dinner monitors, prefects and a few got the 'Jack Petchey awards'. The boys applied for funding from the council during that time and got it, we were so proud of them; they were making a real difference!

Saturday school

Saturday school was another project Debbie and I worked on together. She saw my style and asked whether I would be interested in coming on board; I agreed immediately. This was an opportunity to create engaging lessons from scratch with numeracy and literacy as a focus, and I would be paid for it! I simply could not believe my luck!

Every Saturday I would jump out of bed and complete my chores before I went into the school early. Debbie would always be there preparing the day for the students. I was so enthusiastic. I can't imagine doing that now, working on Saturday, you must be bloody joking, no matter the pay! You think you are appreciated doing something for the school, by looking at the bigger picture, but really you aren't, sorry to say that and when push comes to shove, all that extra work and passion means nothing. Not that you were doing it for praise, but it would have been nice to have acknowledged us for the positive contribution we were making to the community and to the school.

The kids that attended were mainly from primary school, year 5 and 6s; this was a way for the kids to see the school, meet the staff and decide whether to choose this school as a place they would like to come for their secondary education. We were to give lessons but be as informal as possible, so the children would enjoy the lessons and want to come again. Other classes were dance and Information Technology; the children would come in at 9.30 and rotate classes until 12.30, with a break and snack in between.

We had a good team, the admin was done by a lady named Julie, while Sal, who was Head of IT, did the ICT lessons. Omar taught the children street dance and Brian Tobin – remember the Maths teacher? – would do some lessons too, occasionally. Some students from the school would come in and play football on the pitch on Saturday, which Daniel aka Lazy supervised.

We had some kids that had special needs, so I would make sure my lessons were inclusive, engaging and fun, at the same time making the work accessible so all the students of varied abilities and ages within the class would accomplish something.

I enjoyed putting on the classes; it allowed me to be creative. I would put on baking lessons, treasure hunts, logic and mental puzzles, which all involved using numeracy and literacy. Also, the classes were smaller, so I got to really know the students. It was a pleasure! Especially as you would hear the children as they were walking away at the end of the session with their parents, "Look what I learnt or did, Mum!" or "I really had so much fun, Dad!".

***

One day during this Covid period, I thought instead of Hubby getting the bus and having to wear a mask, worrying about whether anyone was going to cough on him, I would pick him up from

Stratford station. I pulled into the slipway in front of the gates, so I could do a three-point turn and park up by the 'pick up point'. The main road is quite narrow and with the introduction of a cycle lane it's hard to do a three-point turn in the road; you cannot do nothing but drive straight forward and pull into the slipway to turn around.

Thankfully, Hubby was already there and just jumped into the passenger front seat. If anyone has been to Stratford station, you will understand that it is a complete mess as in really busy. If you are picking someone up, you have got to do it fast, otherwise it soon becomes a car park. You have two exits from the station. Where I was, was the exit leading to the old town centre where you would find Burger King and Sainsburys, the heart of Stratford before Westfield was built.

In that split second, Hubby jumped into the car, a police car was behind me. I presumed he wanted to go into the double wired gates in front of me; there was a sign saying DO NOT PARK POLICE ENTRANCE.

I mumbled an obscene word under my breath and proceeded to manoeuvre forward with my intention to do a three-point turn as I would have done originally. All of a sudden, the police car lights came on, flashing away with a sense of urgency. I tried to indicate that I was trying to get out of his way and I veered across, giving him space to pass by behind me. I am sure he understood what my intention was, and if not, surely the three white other coppers in his car should have said something.

All of a sudden a chubby-faced white policeman jumps out of the car and rushes up to me:

Unstable police officer: What are you doing? Can't you see my lights flashing!

ICE: I CAN EXPLAIN

He was pointing towards his car, I breathed in and said in a calm voice:

> **Me:** Evening, officer, I was trying to get out of your way.

With experience, I always will greet the police and be as polite as possible, regardless of the situation. I was given that talk years ago by relatives and friends.

> **Unstable police officer:** When you see the lights flashing you pull over, immediately!

> **Me:** But officer, I was just trying to get out of your way.

> **Unstable police officer:** Do you need to go through the gates so I can explain it to you, no parking here!

At that moment, I realised this was a situation that could get out of hand; he thought I was trying to park and did not want to hear what I had to say. I did not have any ID as this was supposed to be a 10min drive, I did not have matching underwear in case, in the extreme, I had to be strip-searched. My hair was not suitable for a mug shot, thus I had a hat on and on top of that I had left my dinner in the oven on a low heat so I really did not want him to take this situation any further. I had things to do, I could imagine me behind those gates and the outcome would not have been pretty for me.

> **Me:** No, officer, I said, breathing deeply, then he said in an angry voice, taking it an unnecessary step further.

> **Unstable police officer:** Can't you read! Can't you read! pointing at the sign.

SUNDAY JUNE 7TH, 2020

I thought I was going to lose the plot, my boy is saying it twice, you know! I did not even look at where he was pointing, I gripped the steering wheel tightly, I was most probably more educated than him, but I was not going to get into any conversation with him, I just looked at his mouth as he rattled on, nodding at the appropriate times, thinking I thought this fool had somewhere to be.

I imagined those other coppers in the car, what were they thinking seeing this scene unfold in front of them? They must have seen my husband get into the car and were still prepared to let this ridiculous conversation continue. I shuddered, thinking what would have happened if I was on my own.

I believed he had had a bad day. The police were under a lot of stress, having to negotiate ever-changing rules and all the time worrying about themselves catching the virus and giving it to their families.

I tried not to take it personally, while I watched him talking, would he have acted this way if I was his shade of skin? Did I look illiterate? All those years of Nigerian elders' voices in my head, saying,

"Education is the most important thing oh! If you want to live under this roof, you better make sure you are working towards being a Doctor, Engineer or Lawyer!" (in Nigerian dialect)

All the years of studying and making my family proud, only to be talked to like a kindergarten child by a person who looks no older than my nephew!

I think when he finally got out of breath and saw I was not engaging with him the way he wanted, he ushered me off.

Unstable police officer: Off you go, let's not meet again.

Me: Thank you, have a good evening, officer!

Again, always end the police interaction in a pleasant way, you never know who he will be stopping next – could be one of my family, student or friends.

I remember driving away from this lunatic, I was absolutely fuming. He had made me feel like nothing, two black adults in the car and neither of us could get a word in; what happened to respectable communication?

I had tears welling up in my eyes but of course I had to dash home to make sure my dinner did not burn, thinking all the while, what could I do to make sure that does not happen again? I must have my ID with me and my hazard lights on while performing the manoeuvre, maybe then I would have felt more confident to push my point forward. I have to still use that space, it has to work for me too, I live here, I cannot be intimidated by a few nutters in the police force, not at this age!

Should I have taken his details to lodge a complaint? At that time, I did not want to prolong the situation any further, I wanted to get away. I remember looking hazily at his serial number, thinking what would happen if I did take it further... absolutely nothing in my opinion!

Looking at the statistics, more than 60% of people stopped by police are from the BAME community, but only 4% go on to make a formal complaint.

During the lockdown, I recall having a conversation with my 16-year-old godson, Emy; we stumbled upon the word BAME, and he asked me what it meant.

"It's a trendy way to refer to people of colour," I said, but then I thought it doesn't really. "It's Black, Asian and Ethnic Minority, no no... Black, Asian and Minority Ethnic." Saying it out loud sounded bizarre, even to me – how can you lump all of those together as one? How was I to explain the logic to someone of that age. The term had just crept up on me over the years and I accepted it myself without thinking too much about it; anyway, Emy was intelligent enough to follow my flow so we were able to continue our conversation, laughing along the way.

I must admit I have never made a complaint, even though I have been stopped by the police countless times over my lifetime. Anything ranging from the wrong thickness of thread on my tyres to thinking my windows were tinted, and the best one was when they pulled me over thinking I was a man!

If I was to have a conversation with him using my app, this is how it would go.

ICE app

Ring ring

Unstable Police Officer: This is PO12345, I stopped you the other day at Stratford station.

Me: Afternoon, Officer, how did you get my number??

I knew immediately who it was; it's not every day you have a confrontation with the police, that had led me to tears.

Unstable police officer: Afternoon, Shola, I got your number from your car details. I had to watch the CCTV footage, that's one of the privileges of being a police officer. I felt I needed to explain my behaviour to you.

Me: Oh ok...

Unstable police officer: Can I just apologise to you about the other day. I have had time to reflect and I could have talked to you more like a human being instead of coming across so aggressive. My colleagues in the car told me I was so red in the face!

Me: I was upset to be honest, but your apology is accepted. Just a word of advice, when you approach people of colour, please be conscious of your tone, that's always appreciated.

Unstable police officer: Yes, I think that comes with experience, I am working on it.

Me: Are you from the local area? As maybe you would have seen that the locals or indeed yourself have used that area to turn their cars around.

Unstable police officer: No, I was drafted in, from just outside London, but getting to know the area like the back of my hands now.

Me: Also, can I suggest that you try to understand how we feel, show empathy, remember you could be the 2nd or 3rd police officer to have stopped me that day or week. It would be great if there was some sort of system that records me being stopped, so when my car approaches, you are informed and let me continue my journey.

Unstable police officer: That's a good idea, will suggest that to the sergeant, but that would have to be a nationwide initiative.

I was on a roll now with suggestions.

SUNDAY JUNE 7TH, 2020

Me: Also, please pull us over for valid reasons, not because you feel like it or we fit a stereotype and when you do, please treat us fairly.

Unstable police officer: Of course, we always try to do that, but we are only human.

Me: I understand that; remember we are human too! We may not be happy about being stopped but don't take that as us not wanting to cooperate.

Unstable police officer: That's understandable.

Me: Also, when you speak to your sergeant, mention recruiting and retaining more ethnic minorities police officers, no offence to you, of course! Because when we see them, we see us in them, we are most likely to apply for those roles. Even better if you are working in mixed racial pairs, so you can bounce off each other in situations, it's a win-win!

Unstable police officer: Ok, Shola, am writing your points down...

Me: And finally, please inform your colleagues to discreetly ask me my gender, if I am being stopped in the future; if they are not sure, not that it matters, it's just embarrassing for me!

Unstable police officer: Of course, that too is understandable. Shola, you have given me a lot to chew over. I will take on board our conversation and use that to become a better police officer for myself, colleagues and the community.

Me: Thanks for calling, PO12345, I appreciate your call and apology.

Gosh, I have given him a lot of work to do, but it felt great getting an apology and getting some suggestions off my chest, I am grateful that he called.

***

Anyway, during this Covid period, I have never felt more safe, despite the experience I just talked about. Coppers were on the street in pairs, actually walking around in my neighbourhood, talking to the residents and explaining the rules and restrictions. Coppers on bikes riding around with their helmets, showing us how it should be done. Coppers in cars and vans zooming all over the borough, looking busy as the lockdown rules continuously change.

Their presence was felt in a positive way around the community. If only this type of policing could continue after Lockdown ends. In the US the shops in the local community offer free coffee and doughnuts to the police, which encourages them to frequent the area and engage with the public. Why can't we introduce this service over here? Better still if some sweet treats were offered along with the cuppa!

Tuesday June 9th, 2020

It was the final day of rest for George Floyd, his final destination was Houston Texas, his home town. His casket was carried by a horse drawn carriage making its way through the city with well-wishers looking on and some following with their fists up in the air. The private funeral was held at The Fountain of Praise Church and of course it was packed with mourners, ranging from family to well-wishers and even celebrities.

A few pastors gave some moving sermons before a male singer took the stage and sang a beautiful version of *'A change gonna come'*. Behind him an artist was painting on a large, black canvas during the singing using white paint and a sponge I think. As I was listening to this beautiful song, I was wondering what the artist was trying to create behind the singer on this black canvas. Freestyling with no template, as the song slowly came to an end, I thought, "You have run out of time, mate, is it supposed to be an abstract piece of art?"

On the last few chords of the song, the artist picks up the canvas and turns it upside down and low and behold the image of George Floyd's face appears, perfectly done! He shows it around for everyone to see what he has created and of course there were grasps of surprise. Even I was taken aback by his talent to create that in such a short period of time, what an amazing picture of George Floyd painted upside down!

One of the speakers, Joe Biden, the presidential candidate, gave a moving speech through Zoom, mostly about America changing and making it right for everyone to be treated equally.

"When there is justice for George Floyd, we will truly be on our way to racial justice and then there will be justice for all." Hopefully, Biden, when you get into power, you will have a hand in making that a reality!

Congressman Al Green said, "We need to have a department of reconciliation to deal with issues relating to the descendants of slavery and segregation and the fact that generations on are still suffering discrimination today."

It was a striking image of unity seeing his family on stage all dressed in white, all quite visibly distressed. His brother Rodney addressed the congregation emotionally saying,

> "Everybody is going to remember him around the world. He is going to change the world."

I totally agree, Rodney, I feel the same, I know something inside me has changed since his death.

The civil rights activist Reverend Al Sharpton rightly said when he was giving the eulogy:

"Unless America comes to terms with their history and the open wounds, how can we heal from them, if you don't recognise the wound?" He added that he is reminded of this each time he writes his name. In reference to George, he said:

> "He was an ordinary brother...he has touched the world...even in a pandemic."

***

Just yesterday, on Monday 8th of June, The House Speaker Nancy Pelosi read George Floyd's name and others who have died at the hands of police brutality and violence.

"We're here to observe that pain," was one of the things she mentioned in her statement.

Then she and the rest of the US Democrats that were present took the knee for 8 minutes and 46 seconds in the Emancipation Hall in front of the media, with the sound of flashing cameras. Afterwards you could see and feel the significance of that moment.

It was a powerful image, not only because they were kneeling, but they each had on beautiful, colourful Kente scarves originally from Ghana around their necks. To be honest, that's what got my attention, because to me it felt they had gone that extra mile to relate to the African American and indirectly to me in the UK.

'George Floyd's Justice in Policing Act of 2020' – this outlines the most ambitious changes to law enforcement by Congress in America for decades. Representative Karen Bass, the chairwoman of the Congressional Black Caucus, who was leading the effort, called it *'transformative'*. The Act was to look at demilitarizing the police and addressing police brutality, which includes banning chokeholds. We will find out whether it has been voted through on the 22nd of June, fingers crossed!

***

Meanwhile during this week in the UK, the statues were cleaned up in Whitehall. The far-right protesters put a call out to their people to protect the statues, the government was nervous and tried to discourage them and Black Lives Matter movement not to protest in Central London, but their pleas fell on deaf ears.

Churchill's statue in London seemed to be a focus; during the week it was boarded up for fear of it being a target during the ongoing protesting.

Some people have a love-hate relationship with Churchill, he was one of our former prime ministers and held a lot of power in his time and respect, but he was also a controversial character. Some say he was a hero for leading us out of war, some say he spent a lot of his time offending people from the black and Asian community. I am quite indifferent to his statue, as I don't have to pass him on a daily basis, thank heavens!

***

Also, yesterday, the statue of Robert Milligan in London Docklands just outside the Museum of London was removed from its plinth with a crane to cheers and clapping. He was another slave trader who owned more than 500 slaves. The Canal and River Trust wanted to *'recognise the wishes of the community'*. I am sure it was done with gritted teeth.

The Email

On the 13th of November 2007 an extraordinary thing happened. I was in between lessons, lost in thought about what resources I needed, when – we shall refrain from naming the person – called out to me from across the playground; he walked briskly up to me and said:

"Have you seen the email?"

"What email?" At that time, I only checked my emails in the mornings and during any rare breaks on the school computer. I was thinking maybe there had been an emergency change to my lessons.

"YOU REALLY NEED TO CHECK YOUR EMAIL ASAP," he said and I could see from the look on his face he was serious.

I rushed to the room my lesson was in before the students arrived at the door and logged on to the computer and quickly opened my

TUESDAY JUNE 9TH, 2020

emails and skimmed the inbox. Nothing new... I tried to keep focused during that lesson, but all I kept thinking was:

"What email was he talking about? And what were its contents?"

As soon as the lesson finished, I went looking for someone who we won't say their name, and he told me apparently someone from IT had gone into everyone's emails and retrieved and destroyed the email.

"That's why I couldn't find it!" I exclaimed

He then handed me a printed copy. I could not believe this person had managed to get a physical copy. Absolute genius! I thought as I read it over quickly trying to find out what all the fuss is about.

> Now, could you solve the problem of difficult staff. Oh yes Mr E, you're not the only one who suffers from this. We all have a heavy burden to bear when it comes to people – an admin officer who shouts at everyone when I'm not around, a science technician who cannot come to work because it's too cold at the bus stop, an admin assistant who refuses to take minutes as it's not in the job description, a TA who only communicates via sick certificates, a cover supervisor who's probably on drugs...now, onto the teachers...
>
> Ha, ha – you've got to keep laughing – it's the only way. Just think of their miserable, petty little lives where work is the most important thing – how sad is that. And then revel in your glorious fortune – healthy, good home, nice wife, lots of travel, lovely garden, nice family, good hobbies etc.

Shelley – remember that woman who dealt with the finances of the school – had written this email to her husband that morning (during work hours on the school's computer, I must add) and instead of emailing just him, she managed to email the whole school. In the email, she expresses the way she felt about seven members of staff.

She did not mention any names, but it was quite obvious who she was talking about.

"Really! Why is she being such a spoilt brat!" The more I read it the more I realised out of the two cover supervisors, it's likely with people's perceptions they will presume it's me, due to the black person stereotype. I suddenly realised the implications of this email on me and my reputation around the school and the colour drained from my face.

I said cheers to the person who had given it to me and rushed to see Daniel aka Lazy.

I asked him what he felt about it; I don't know why I bothered!

He just shrugged and said, "What's the big deal?"

He didn't understand how it impacted on me; why am I not surprised at his reaction?

I was upset and aggravated, because the staff had started making jokes at me regarding the email. Andy, the head of Year 7 said, "When are you giving up your day job, Shola?" and everyone around laughed.

Staff in the science department had been talking about it too, as the email referred to a science technician, who was off sick. One of the Learning Support Assistant, Khalid said, "I am shocked that such an email has been sent around the school!", and jokingly said on the day, "I hear you are the person to buy a score from!"

I couldn't believe this was happening to me!

Shelley had dissed the majority of the staff in the school, at least it felt that way in the staff room when whispers were swirling around. "Who does she think she is?"

"I wonder what will happen to her?"

"Bloody hell! I would not want to be in her shoes."

I spoke to Charlotte on several occasions that day, and she assured me that the matter was being dealt with and would be revealed in the morning briefing.

Later that day, all staff received a letter from Charlotte. But, that did not stop me being at the receiving end of jokes, which even though I shrugged off, I did not find it amusing and I obviously did not want to be associated with illegal drugs. I think in the morning we were given some vague explanation during the daily briefing that Shelley would be taking some time off.

To be honest, I would not want to be in her position. I thought if that was me, I would have to resign from the school immediately surely, I would be so embarrassed! On the day the email was sent, Charlotte appeared to go with Shelley everywhere. I remember thinking this was strange that the head teacher would take such a personal interest in one of her staff. I was later to find out, that they were in fact, personal good friends and had worked in a previous school together. She also did this on Shelley's return to work after the email incident, Ms Robinson the head teacher aka the miniature close protection guard!

Aha! It all made sense now!

On Shelley's return after a few days off (am sure with pay), Daniel and I were called into Charlotte's office. I had been summoned, and thought I had done something wrong, until I walked into the office and saw Shelley sitting there. You could see that she had been crying and when she saw us, on cue she turned it up a level, wiping her eyes and sniffing. She apologised and gave us written apologies as well. I was quite upset with the situation for several reasons:

We had been summoned to Charlotte's office, without any prior notice, so could not prepare any form of response or have support.

I was not happy that Shelley had smeared my name for no reason and all I was getting was a measly apology! What about the effect on my reputation?

And finally, she was still working in the school; I knew if I had done that, I would have been out of the door in a shot!

Life at school continued as before, or so I thought, even though I felt at the time, my relationship with Charlotte had been tarnished. I put it down to my reaction to the email. I started to notice how she would exclude me out of conversations with other staff members, for example, when doing gate duty; she would stand in front of me, or speak over me, when I was talking.

On one occasion I was speaking to a member of staff regarding a student, and before I finished, Charlotte interrupted and said the student was receiving some counselling. I remember thinking, *'That's not very professional'*, firstly butting into a conversation and secondly mentioning a private intervention, but she is the Head teacher after all, and I could clearly see, she did not seem to like hearing my voice or sharing the same air as me. Looking back, I feel her treatment of me was a power trip, she wanted to see me cringe and be uncomfortable and feel the lowest of the lowest, which she succeeded in doing.

Another example of her rudeness, was when I was doing my lunch duty as usual in the dining hall. Walking around, making sure things were running smoothly. I was talking to some monitors about lunch duty and Charlotte approached me and said, in front of the monitors:

"Les has to go and fix a broken window, go and cover the gate, while he is doing that."

I was not surprised that there was no *'please'* or that her voice was hostile. She couldn't even address me by name or give me an explanation as to why I had to do it. I was quite embarrassed really, because she had spoken to me in that way in front of the students, so in order to hide my embarrassment, I quickly said:

"Ok, Miss," and hurriedly left the dining hall, to go to the gate to meet Les the caretaker.

***

TUESDAY JUNE 9TH, 2020

I started to name Charlotte *'Stone'*, as that's how I felt about her and her treatment of me; she seemed to have no soul or feelings, like a block of ice, absolutely nothing can get through to the core!

I just could not understand this. Unbelievably she had three kids of her own, but did not behave like a mother, by showing any empathy; she came across to me as emotionless, an empty vessel. I just wanted to be treated professionally like a fellow human being, where I worked, by this woman, was that too much to ask??

I simply found her behaviour distasteful; after all, we, the members of staff, had to lead by example. If this was happening to one of the students in school, we as a society would all surely jump on it and stop it in its tracks, but as adults, it seemed this behaviour was simply acceptable.

I don't think I ever saw her in trousers, she was a skirt, dress or suit woman, who covered a lot of ground when walking. She just seemed to be so unapproachable, even though she had or should have no presence, she magically did, and marched around the school with swirls of confidence. I feel physically sick just having to think about her. In all my years of security where I felt empowered in that environment, then coming and working here, being disrespected and not being treated as a human being is something I never imagined that I would ever experience in my career or life.

Just writing this and having to think about this person is making me queasy, need to take a moment…

As time progressed, Grant Bulmuo, Head of Maths, requested me more in the Maths department. I guess he saw and appreciated my skills, he could trust me as he had watched me over time. Grant was apparently a Pastor and actually led a church. He was always well presented but an extremely reflective, quiet man with a shiny, bald egg-shaped head. He wore rimmed glasses and always looked in deep thought, there was always a slight hesitation before he spoke as if he was composing his words. I remember being proud that a black man, from Africa, held that role and wondered what he had done to reach that level.

I remember one time he had a sudden death in the family, all the way in Ghana. He had to leave suddenly and even though there were other members in the Maths department, I was trusted to take some of his classes when he was away.

On his return, the feedback he gave me was that the students had understood what I had taught them and he thanked me for marking the students' books, plus keeping an eye out generally for them. I was genuinely chuffed, of course; at the time I kind of hung on every word he said. Here was a black man who was lucky enough to be in a senior position in the Maths department. I wanted him to mentor me informally and any positive feedback from him I lapped up.

***

The career advisor part was ongoing, Chris was coming into the school less and less, and giving me more tasks to do with the boys. I didn't mind as I could see it was necessary and no one else was available to take it on.

At some point in time, I was given a budget of nearly £500 by the school to spend on books. I remember I took this so seriously, asking the students what they would like to see and asking Mary the Librarian to make space in a prominent area that would catch the students' attention.

Mary was the stern librarian; she was a Caribbean light-skinned lady with natural, long afro hair. She really made the library a destination spot, she had it on lockdown and the students respected the space and of course the books. Mary kept to her word and allowed me to display the books and supported the boys to read not just the title but the contents.

TUESDAY JUNE 9TH, 2020

    I loved seeing the books arrive. I ordered more than thirty books like: How to write a CV, Start up your own Business, Directory of University and Colleges, Dental school, Great answers to tough interview questions, and others like Bullying, Family break ups, Teenagers' Survival Guide.

***

Newham was a borough that had a high level of unemployment. Some of these students experienced real poverty and were hard-core with ideas of just wanting to make money "the fast way". Influenced by the popularity of music videos, featuring designer clothes, cars and women, making it all seem so easy to achieve.

    Some of the students' parents were either single-parents working every hour of the day, or parents who worked unsociable hours. There were normally younger siblings in the picture that the students had to look after in the evenings or pick up from neighbouring schools. Some parents didn't want to engage with the school system, as there always seemed to be constant negative feedback about their child.

    That was not the parents' immediate concerns, paying the rent and electricity were their daily worries and putting food on the table.

    On occasions when I would talk to a group of boys, especially from the 'Black and Asian community', I would pose the same questions, over and over:

    What do you want to do in the future? What are your plans?

    One of the common answers I would get in unison would be "A drug dealer!" then massive laughter.

    "Miss, that's a no brainer!"

    "Why?" I would reply.

    "Cause, Miss, you get the girls, money and cars!" Loud laughter and cheers of agreement.

I understood why they felt that way, as on the surface it all looked good, until they got caught.

"Do you know once you get a criminal record, it's difficult to get a job?"

"I am not gonna get caught, Miss!" More laughter, but not so loud this time.

"It only takes the once, then you are labelled, son," I said with a solemn look on my face.

I would expand on that, it was the first time a lot of them thought about the implications of their proposed illegal actions.

"Also, you will find it difficult to get into certain countries; I am sure you want to travel around the world?" I could see they were now thinking about it.

"And the worst scenario, you could end up in jail or sadly dead."

I was being dramatic, but sometimes you need to be extreme to get their attention. We were living in the time of knife crime, you couldn't be a young black man in this area and not know about the *'postcode wars'*. They needed to know there were other options that were outside what they could have imagined for themselves.

"There are legitimate ways to succeed, especially as you all have potential, you all have to think and make a plan. I will help you if you want?"

Then I would show them courses available in local Colleges or apprenticeships, then see what grades were required and finally see how they could attain those grades. This meant focusing on handing in good quality coursework and revising for exams. You could see that they started to believe in themselves. Also highlighting other skills like leadership, working in a team, being organised etc. It's not always the academic qualifications!

"Can you imagine how you would feel, once you achieve your goals…legally?"

Saturday school

Saturday school was going well and our reputation in the local community was really good, following feedback we had received, which meant Year 6 students were actually considering attending our school in Year 7. We had recently been formally assessed and the feedback we received was great, the kids were actually making progress in our sessions. We had plans to expand on what we were doing and to increase our numbers. I was excited by this but still wanted to go on this TA course so I could feel I was properly qualified for the job and of course receive my correct wage.

Learning Mentor

Around this time Daniel aka Lazy started to shadow a Learning Mentor called Eric who worked alongside Debbie. I thought, 'Wow, he has been given another opportunity to increase his wages and have some sort of career progression!'

I was feeling forgotten about. Daniel was constantly on training courses relating to being a Learning Mentor and I was practically left doing the Cover Supervisor work alone. Eric had a reduced timetable and would be leaving the role soon, hence the need to fill this role. When he finally left, a temporary Learning Mentor was employed by the school, by the name of Mary.

More career work

Mick could not attend a one-day course aimed at the *'Career Advice providers in schools'*, he felt confident in sending me in his place and for me to give him feedback on my return. Mick was adamant that I went to represent him. I don't even think he had time to clear it with Charlotte aka Stone; either way I was eager to go. It was held near Romford in East London, so I just hopped on to the Overground train.

All the participants were really nice and as I took notes and listened to the presentation, I thought, with all the work I had done with the career advice, it would be a good idea to go for further training so I could provide a better service to the students, especially as the funding for having a Career Advisor from Connexions was coming to an end.

I discussed this with Mick on my return. He thought it was a good idea as I was doing a lot of work, and it would release him to focus on his other roles, he said he would mention it next time at the SLT meeting.

Soon after that, Mick and I organised a Careers fair, where we invited different organisations like the Army, local businesses, Colleges and Sixth Forms from the local area. It was a successful event and a lot more students applied for further education. Shortly after this event, the issue of me attending courses on Career advice came up at an SLT meeting, but Mike was told by Stone that she did not think it was necessary for me to attend those courses. Can you imagine!

That one child...

Some students just did not understand why they had to be in school. In those cases, it was an uphill struggle to try and get them to do any work, let alone sit down for one hour at a time, without disrupting the whole class. The significance of education just went over some of the boys' heads; I would at every opportunity stress the importance of doing well in whatever career path they chose to follow. Especially, pointing out that they were competing for the same jobs or college places as every other young person in the UK.

Some of them thought school was always going be there, like a welcome shelter. It came as a shock that they had to leave school and fend for themselves. I would see some students coming back to the school after they had graduated. They were looking for support and I could see the longing in their eyes to be back in a safe, caring environment. Especially those students who didn't do as well as they should have.

In every class there is always that one student, who is like that and would rather be home. That student has authority over the class and like a shot, they could click a finger and disrupt the whole lesson, either by saying something controversial or acting like a comedian.

One of those such students was a boy called Aaron in Year 10; he was a mixed-race boy with afro length hair which he tied in a ponytail. He thought he was a bad boy as he had a reputation around the area. He was quite intelligent, and had a sharp tongue, so most of the other students looked up to him.

Our first meeting was a Maths class. He took an instant dislike to me, because he wanted his normal teacher and did not want me to be there. I was always surprised with the response I got from some of the boys about my presence, how could they be so rude to me?

I heard him say, to a smaller boy next to him, "Who the hell is this clown?" The boy just shrugged his shoulders.

I proceeded to introduce myself, and dish out worksheets his teacher had left; Aaron sat down and put his feet up on the table in front of him. I must admit, he un-nerved me, because of his aggressive nature. I gave him a stern look, but it was only until I threatened to get Senior Management that he reluctantly moved his feet. He hated backing down in front of everyone and he threw me dirty looks for the rest of the lesson. Swearing and cursing me under his breath, just loud enough for me to hear but low enough for him to deny it, I took the stand just to ignore him and got through the lesson, thank God!

I tried to get through to him in subsequent lessons, but to no avail; he would walk away from me if I tried to initiate a conversation with him. When he realised I was still around months later and he had heard through the grapevine that I had the students' best interests at heart, it was only then when he was in his final term of Year 11, did he nod my way and I acknowledged this by nodding back. No words were ever spoken, but we had come to a truce between us and that was enough for me!

He was like that with a lot of the staff; he just did not engage with authority or the educational system and did not see the importance of it. Such a shame we could not reach him, as I am sure he would have been good in some sort of apprenticeship scheme, by being mentored. Unfortunately, he left with hardly any qualifications. I often wonder now how his life turned out.

Sometimes you would give some form of responsibility to such students, like handing out books or writing the date on the board. It seemed the other students listened to such students and they were indirectly called "leader". In my opinion once you get those sort of students on your side, everything else was child's play. If you were not lucky enough to be able to do that, then you definitely would have a battle on your hands.

On the flip side, Hassan came to England from India in Year 8; he could not speak hardly any English and he lacked confidence. He was placed in a lower ability class, where he found it hard to work, as he was surrounded by disruptive students. I met him when he was in Year 10, he would always ask me for extra help and do the work to the best of his ability.

I remember him coming to the Careers room for advice and for assistance in filling out college application forms. His predicated grades were Ds and Es, but he strongly wanted to go into the medical field. Due to his hard work, he achieved higher grades than predicted. He had also started working to support himself in a warehouse, I think packing goods, but he would always turn out clean and promptly ready to learn for school. When he came back to the school after he graduated to say "thank you" to me and other members of staff, I was choked with tears of pride, he looked so smart in his suit and tie. He had worked so hard and was now in college, with such a

TUESDAY JUNE 9TH, 2020

bright future ahead of him...

Thursday June 11th 2020

I was watching the show *'Question Time'* for my weekly political community conversation on the BBC.

Bernardine Evaristo was on the panel which made it even more interesting as she wrote the acclaimed novel *'Girl, Woman, Other'*.

I remember when she jointly won the Booker prize in 2019 with Margaret Atwood who wrote *'The Testaments'*. I was so enraged by the fact that the panel couldn't decide between the two of them. When researching, I found that this had happened twice before, but in 1993, the rules were changed so it didn't happen again.

Margaret had won it before – why couldn't they just let Bernardine take the crown solo?

I can imagine the conversation around the table by the decision makers:

"We can't possibly let her win… she is a black woman!"

"Well, her work is so good, we just can't ignore it!"

"Oh dear, we have a dilemma, what do we do, what do we do?"

Well, we found out, didn't we? They decided to break the rules again and share the prize, go figure!

It's always so refreshing to see black women as part of the panel on Question Time. She looked good with her tell-tale colourful head scarf and sounded so confident when talking about slavery and its history.

When asked about the timely discussion on statues, she said she *'absolutely relished'* seeing the toppling of Edward Colston. She added that campaigners had tried for years to get it removed or a plaque put on the statue with further information about him.

The sales of her book have soared, she is the first Black woman to top the paperback fiction chart. I am so proud of you for making it, Bernardine, you continue to pave the way for the rest of us to follow!

News outlets

One of my favourite choices of media is the radio. I just heard recently that the BBC are promising more money towards drama and shows promoting black people, in other words *'Diversity programmes'*. I welcomed this of course!

But I personally hope that they actually give more opportunities for disadvantaged students to gain work experience for real job roles within the establishment. There is so much talent in inner city schools, but I have never seen a programme designed to attract them from grassroots with proper incentives so they could remain focused on the role and not look for money elsewhere for their basic needs. It seemed only the rich and influential families can support their own children to take up such opportunities at the BBC.

Don't get me wrong, I love the BBC – being able to listen to a show live, with no interruptions of adverts, absolutely priceless! I especially enjoy listening to BBC London, the show called *'The Scene'* had diverse presenters like feisty comedian Judi Love and the infectious Salma El-Wardany and who could do without Uncle Eddie Nester? Doing his entertaining with deep conversations during his drive time shows. I must not forget *'The Night Watchman'* Dotun Adebayo with his huge expanse of knowledge and soothing voice, who to be honest should be at the table, but I wonder how many people who are the decision makers are people of colour at the BBC? Are the individuals around the table reflecting diversity?

I just have to take a look at the backdrop in the background during the intro of the BBC news at the actually newsroom. It's open plan within a large area, I can roughly count how many people of colour I see, wait for it… hardly any! Which is a real shame, as I want to see my licence fee representing people like me.

A report on career progression of staff from Black, Asian and minority ethnic background at the BBC has been put in place to deal with the issue raised and much more.

"Today's report is a huge step forward. There's no question of whether we will implement it. We will. This is a great opportunity. We will grasp it," said Lord Tony Hall, Director-General of the BBC.

"We will be keeping an eye on the progress of that, Tony; even though you are leaving the role in the summer, make sure your replacement keeps the focus. Maybe a person of colour for the role perhaps?"

2008
Learning mentor role

Mary, the temporary Learning Mentor, fitted right into the school and most importantly she was qualified and had experience. The students took to her quickly, so when the post was formally advertised months later, everyone was surprised that Daniel aka Lazy got the job. Even though I was happy for him, I remember thinking, why was I not given such an opportunity?

Or was it just that Daniel was lucky to have gone on the Teaching Assistant course, got back pay and then managed to get training for the Learning Mentor role and got the job too which was a higher salary of course!

He was working alongside Debbie now! I just could not believe how much support and opportunities he had been given to be able to grow. Why could I not have even a slice of this?

Dining hall incidents

Just recently after that, Debbie and I were talking in the dining hall about giving the boys seconds, this was around 1.30pm.

Charlotte aka Stone came right up to us and said to Debbie, "I am leaving now, at least you have Leslie Baker with you," and she walked off.

Debbie was surprised and puzzled, because she was often left in the dining room with me. She did not understand why Stone felt the need to make that statement, as there was no need for it, and why did she not mention my name. Did Stone not see me, standing right there?

I just turned away to hide my embarrassment, because I was used to experiencing that type of treatment from her, even though Leslie was there, she was not in hearing distance of the conversation. I liked Leslie, she was an English Teacher and in her previous life, a nurse. She had five children and had a caring nature about her. I am sure if she had heard what Stone said, she would have been puzzled too.

I explained to Debbie, it was for my benefit, that it was Stone's way to make me feel insignificant. Soon after Stone left the dining hall, Leslie followed after, leaving Debbie and I to finish the shift as usual.

***

Drama incident

One of the reasons I prepared my own resources, was to have something for the students to do during a lesson, if the teacher or department had not pre-planned work for the students. This happened so frequently that I was getting frustrated, as it was hard for me to do my job properly and no amount of highlighting this issue with my managers seemed to change anything.

Sometimes it's unavoidable, as it's an emergency absence, but if it's longer than a day, then as a cover supervisor it's hard to keep the students engaged, as they want to do the subject timetabled, which is understandable.

One such incident was when I was covering Willie Deighan's Drama class. He was a pleasant enough member of staff with a leadership role and unfortunately had a back injury. It was obvious he was going to be out of school for a while – this was a few days into his absence, and I had already complained to the Head of Drama, that the cover provided for his classes was not sufficient. I understood that Willie had other priorities at that time, like dealing with the pain that comes with such an injury.

I had to take his feisty Year 9 class for a double session and again no cover from Mr Deighan was left. The Head of Department was nowhere to be found. "Typical," I thought! Once the students saw me, there was a lot of groaning and muttering. I explained, after I calmed them down, that even though I knew they were missing their teacher, any work provided still had to be done and behaviour still had to be acceptable. I then whipped out some Drama worksheets from my resources for them to be getting on with.

One of them said, "But, Miss, this is a drama lesson and we want to practise our role-playing skills, not writing!" A lot of the boys chimed in and said, "Yes, Miss, we want to practice!"

I took a deep breath, because they had a point – the worksheets had nothing to do with what the students were currently working on, so I said, "You can work in your groups for ten minutes in the drama room, while I look for any relevant work that I can find from your teacher".

The students were happy with this, and as I stood by the door letting them into the practice room, I said in an elevated voice, "If any of you lot misbehave, everyone has to come back into the classroom". I got some grunts as a few of them replied. The main classroom had another room attached to it, through a door which was the practice room; it had its own access to the main corridor in which you could get back to the main classroom. It was painted black from top to toe, even the windows; I think for better effect during rehearsals of plays; it was carpeted from wall to wall, with nothing but a table by the side of the wall, a whiteboard and a selection of dimmer switches for the lights.

I could not find anything more relevant in my stash, so decided to give them posters to design, based on the work they had done in previous drama classes. Some students predictably finished their work and after delaying them as long as I could, by giving them further tasks, I finally resigned and let a few in to practise again.

I initially kept the door open, so I could see what was happening, but the noise was too loud, and the other students were trying to finish their work, so I closed the door and locked it, so the students would not keep coming back into the lesson through that door. I was not really worried because the practice room door was opened to the corridor so they could come back to the classroom that way. Looking back now, I would never do that again.

All of a sudden, I heard a loud cry, and as I attempted to open the door, I could see that the boys had turned off the lights, and were play fighting by practising wrestling moves. The student who was crying was embarrassed because all of his classmates were staring and laughing at him. I quickly put on the lights and rushed to him. He did not want my help and when I tried to comfort him, he angrily swore at me and hastily got up, marched into the classroom sniffling and sat down.

I quickly got everyone back into the main classroom which took the focus away from him and got the boys to positively comment on each other's work. I looked out of the corner of my eye and I could see he was listening, the sniffling had subsided, my watch said one minute to the bell. "Thank God," I thought.

Once the last student had left the classroom, I approached the sniffling student, and asked whether he needed to see the nurse. He mumbled that he was ok, grabbed his bag, slid past me and was out of the door before I could say "boo!". I was going to find out what had actually happened in the practice room and to let him know I did not appreciate his colourful language, even if he was hurt.

I approached him later in the day to find out whether he was ok, but before I spoke, he had dashed off again. I wrote an incident report, laying out what I ascertained from the other students. Apparently, the sniffling student had attempted to jump onto another student, missed and injured himself, hence the explanation of his embarrassment and laughter from his co-students. I placed a copy in Mr Deighan and the Head of Department's pigeonhole, a requirement that was expected of staff when an incident like this happens.

On Mr Deighan's return, he approached me and I reiterated what had happened, even though he had a copy of the incident in his pigeonhole; also I pointed out the lack of cover. He apologised for that and said, "Thanks for improvising, Shola, I didn't know I would be off school for that long."

I smiled and said, "No problem, if you get time, can you have a word with that student about the swearing?"

"Yeah, I am surprised and disappointed with him, I will be chasing him up on that," he replied. I believed him; after all, he was a member of the SLT.

On the following Monday, I received a letter in my pigeonhole, stating that an informal investigation was going to take place on the Friday regarding the incident in the drama room – a complaint had been received from the sniffling student.

It went on to further say that if I wanted to come to this investigation with a friend or a trade union representative I could. It took a while for the information in the letter to register in my head. "A complaint? An investigation, why? And why do I need a union representation?" I thought the matter had been dealt with and the student had refused any medical attention at the time. I expected Mr

Deighan to have seen through his bluff, as it was obvious that he was not pleased about being rebutted for his swearing.

I spoke to Seamus Fox about the situation, as I valued his opinion. Remember Seamus? He was one of the gents who interviewed me; he is a white teacher with an Irish background, who was like a brother from another mother.

He worked with low achieving students among other roles. I have to mention his classroom – he had one of those portable classrooms in the playground. It was simply chaos in there, papers on every surface, stationery beneath the papers, games and large different coloured papers in the corners, cabinets overflowing etc. I itched to organise it, but resisted as he would always say "It's organised chaos, Shola!". The students seemed to love being separate from the other students as there was a relaxed vibe about Seamus's room, he had their respect and they managed to learn with his unique style of teaching within their surroundings.

He was the sort of person you could chill in the pub for hours with, engaging in stimulating conversations and not know where the time went. Anyway, I asked him for advice as he saw that I was looking perplexed in the staff room. He asked me whether I belonged to a union.

I replied inquisitively, "No, should I join one?"

He looked at me surprised. "Everyone is in a union, Shola; you never know what situation you could end up in!"

"Hmm… if I join now, will someone from the union come to this meeting on Friday with me?"

He pondered for a minute and said he would be prepared to come with me, as I might not be able to sort out the union before then. I was really encouraged with his proposed support and I got on with finding out what unions were out there.

Drama meeting

At the meeting held in Mr Deighan's room, which was next door to Shelley's office, I could see that Mr Deighan was surprised that Seamus Fox had accompanied me. I acknowledged and apologised that I should not have locked the door, but I kept on emphasising that had the cover been sufficient, I would not have been in that situation.

Even though Mr Deighan tried to avoid my attempts, Seamus kept reminding him about the lack of cover, and eventually Mr Deighan ended the meeting. I was in shock, because it seemed he was trying to make a mountain out of a mole hill and discipline me in some form or other. If Seamus had not been there and kept drawing his attention to the lack of cover that he himself had failed to provide, I am sure I would have been halfway out of the school.

This incident really woke me up to protecting myself properly, after the email incident and now this. After asking around I found out that most of the non-teaching staff belonged to Unison, so I contacted them and was told that the payments would come directly out of my pay. I was to inform my local branch if I needed any assistance with any work-related matters in future.

***

Around June, Charlotte aka Stone approached me in the dining hall in front of students again and said, "You will not be required to work in the dining hall anymore; you will be in the playground during the lunch period, from now on…"

I thought, what did I do wrong? After 18 months of hard work in the dining hall, I waited for an explanation, but none came from her. I did not know what else to say and as I did not want to cause a scene in front of the students, so, I simply said, "Ok, Miss", and started doing my lunch duty in the playground the following day. I knew at that stage I had to face the fact that Charlotte aka Stone did not like or respect me and I didn't know what to do about it!

New recruit

Since Daniel aka Lazy had become a Learning Mentor, I was doing the cover work on my own in combination with agency workers. After a few months, the school finally employed Cherelle Millington as the second Cover Supervisor. She was so refreshing and came into the job with so much enthusiasm and an infectious laugh, it reminded me of me when I first started at Rokeby. I never saw her wage slip but I think she was employed on scale 4 with no mention of a TA course or the possibility of moving up to scale 5. Of course I told her to join Unison, but she didn't feel the need to at that time.

Cherelle was black, young and energetic, eager to do a good job and happy to be able to provide for her young son. Because of my busy schedule, I didn't spend as much time with her as I should have, but I tried to answer all her questions and advise her on developing her own resources. During this time Grant realised that I had never had an official lunch schedule, ever since I started the job, he insisted that I have lunch during the lunch period or during period 4 or 5. This was laughable that he was so concerned about me having a lunch break after how many years of working there!

What was funnier is that he didn't inform Wendy or any other staff members, doing the rota, so Cherelle and me were still expected to do it, and if we were not at our allocated position during the lunch time nine times out of ten, we would be hunted down and asked to do it. I was tired of trying to explain and would redirect those staff members to Grant, but the message never seemed to get through.

Stop and search incident

One evening as Debbie and I were walking the boys from the BPAP out of the school after another purposeful session (they were in groups of two or three) when we saw two police vans coming down one of the side streets. This was not a strange sight as we had a police station at the top of the road. But all of a sudden the vans screeched up to us and stopped suddenly; it was like slow motion, because I could see the vans approaching, and in my mind, I knew they would stop the boys. I thought the boys were in uniform and it's clear that they were just leaving school premises and of course we were thankfully there to clarify anything. The side and back doors of the vans opened simultaneously and at least ten officers spilled out of the vans.

A sinking feeling came over me as they rushed towards us with force, aggression and determination.

In that split second, Debbie and I looked at each other; we both were alarmed and spoke loudly and pointed our hands at the boys. I felt intimidated and knew that we would not be listened to, but we had to try.

"They are with us, we all just came out of school!" We pointed to the gates, but they just ignored us.

"If you want to stop the boys, let me help, as you are appearing extremely aggressive right now," Debbie said to a policeman next to her.

They had gotten to the boys already, one particular boy was on his own, Dolton a quiet, polite, dark skinned boy in Year 10 and words were exchanged between him and a group of armed police men and women. From what I overheard, they wanted him flat-faced on the ground and understandably he was not happy about it. He informed them in an elevated voice that he had medical issues.

They ignored him and in a blink of an eye more than five officers wrestled him down to the dirty concrete ground and remained on top of him. He kept on shouting "Get off me, you are hurting me!" and "I can't breathe!".

It was very distressing to watch and there was nothing I could do. One of the English Teachers, Tracy Ward, who was a snotty white woman came from the English block. I thought, "Thank God, a white person and senior management too, maybe they will listen to her!"

Instead, I remember her hurriedly coming towards the scene saying "What has he done now?". I could not believe it! She made me so angry that she had already concluded that it was the Dolton's fault, Debbie and I just looked at her, I think Debbie said quite bluntly to her to keep her nose out of it.

We were trying to keep the rest of the students calm as well as appealing to the policemen to get off of him, as he clearly was not a danger, had no weapons and was not resisting.

"Get off of him, can't you see he is struggling to breathe?" Debbie repeatedly said. We were responsible for these students, what would we tell his parents? People started to come out of their houses and gather around, watching this chaos unfold. All the other boys were lined up against the fence, having their bags and pockets turned inside out.

"He has asthma, get off of him!" Debbie said.

We were all looking on, we could see Dolton was struggling to breathe, we could not believe this, adult men and women were literally on a defenceless child, it was distressing to witness this behaviour. We continued to protest and Debbie moved closer towards Dolton, to see whether she could tell him to relax, anything, other than just doing nothing.

"Ma, step away," the police woman said and went to push Debbie away.

"Don't touch me!" Debbie said clearly, but with a deadly stare.

"This is going crazy," I thought, they are going to end up arresting Debbie, if we are not careful.

I was disappointed that the boys had to experience this hostile treatment; we needed to deescalate this situation and fast. They were no other members of staff around, just Debbie and I trying to reassure the other boys, not sure whether this was real or in the movies. I was frantically looking around for any staff member (obviously not Tracy again!), ideally a white person from senior management, maybe they would calm the police down so they would listen, but unfortunately no other staff were around.

Debbie informed the police that we had a resident Police Officer at the school, and it would be better if he handled the situation as he already knew the boys and would be able to calm the situation down. He had an office within the school, he was quite visible, interacting with the boys before, during and after school, and his door was open for questions from the boys. It took time for the relationship and trust to grow between him and the boys. But it did! He played football with them and showed them that he cared. I felt it did a lot of good, him being there for the boys within the school, intervening and advising before situations got out of hand.

This was such a time! We called him frantically and Brad was on the scene soon after. By then, more neighbours and locals were hovering around, but unfortunately the Police Officers who had started it would not back down to save face, and in the end they insisted that Dolton was taken to Forest Gate Police Station.

We informed Dolton's family – understandably they were in hysterics, especially Dolton's mother. Debbie went straight to the Police Station and I joined her later. It was hours later before he was released without charge, seeing him for the first time since his detainment he looked aged and I knew something had changed in him forever.

"Did that just happen?" Debbie and I said. What was the purpose for all that stress? Nothing was found, nobody was charged. It was simply a low budget horror movie for the local residents and an everlasting experience that the boys, ourselves and certainly Dolton will never forget.

Debbie spoke to Stone the next day, expecting her to be outraged and follow it up, and of course, she did nothing. Debbie later filed a complaint about the way the boys were treated and the behaviour of the woman officer, but again nothing came out of it. I am not sure whether Dolton's family complained; I would not blame them if they did.

We later found out that the police had been drafted in from all parts of the country and were just driving around, but none was from the local area. If the police were from the local area, they would have known this was a school that had activities going on after school and how to deal with those black students in a less aggressive way. We, as adults were there, the boys did what they were told because we had advised them to and given them the talk during our sessions – what more could they have done?

Considering it was a multi-cultural area, it would have been good to have officers that represented that in the van that day, maybe then they might not have had such an aggressive approach to a bunch of boys in uniform coming out of the school, or better still liaise with our resident police officer Brad.

It was for reasons like this Debbie and I set up the sessions after school, we were able to talk about what happened as a group afterwards. The boys were really angry and frustrated about the police's behaviour. We were able to role play how to react if that type of situation happened again and reminded the boys to remain calm, polite, cooperative and ask for identification if needed. Finally, a copy of the search report if possible, we wanted the boys to trust the police and have a positive relationship with them.

***

Over the years the respect for the police in the UK from the public has deteriorated, due to the few who use excessive force, are corrupt, abuse the rules and are not being held accountable etc. We the public need to be able to trust the police – after all they are a police service not a police force for all races.

We need the police to be respected when they are called to carry out their roles, but it's a two-way process. My worries sometimes with the haste of recruiting officers at such a quick rate is that those new recruits don't have enough life experience for the role and are not fit enough. There are very few criteria for joining the police now, over 18, lived in the UK for more than three years and no criminal record – that's it, near enough!

Back in the day it seemed that the police had experience and more presence. When they attended an incident or engaged with the public, they had the confidence and were able to use their initiative to deescalate situations without the use of excessive force.

***

Anyway, during the beginning of the lockdown, Stratford station was turned into a one-way system. Entry through the Westfield side and exit towards the old town centre, with British Transport Police manning the entrance and exits at the beginning of the lockdown, expecting to see your work ID, you wearing a face mask and asking you the reasons why you needed to travel at that time.

"Don't travel on public transport unless it's essential" is what we constantly heard on the daily TV briefings

"Go to work only if you have to, otherwise work from home."

"Only key workers allowed to travel during peak times."

I would not want to be in the position of enforcing those rules; people were already hypersensitive.

September 2008

September went by and nothing.

I found out all the details of the course and printed out all the necessary paperwork, I had everything ready, put me on the course for crying out loud! There was a deadline so I kept going to Grant to get the papers signed so I could start. I was frustrated as I did not understand why the school would not put me on this course promptly and automatically. It was stressing me out seriously and I didn't know what else to do.

Eventually, late September Grant said to me, as he could see my frustration, "I have not got time to contact her, why don't you call and book a place as time is running out, fill in the relevant paperwork, so I can sign it and give it to Charlotte to counter-sign."

"No problem, I will get onto that!" I replied, and before you could say 'Abracadabra', I emailed Deborah on 4th of October 2008.

> Hi Deborah,
>
> I am a Cover Supervisor at Rokeby School, and I am interested in the Teacher Assistant course.
>
> I have been working in the role above for the past 18 months, and feel this is the right way forward in my career.
>
> I understand the course might have started already, but I would be able to catch up on any work missed.
>
> I have the backing of the school, who have said to contact you for an application form to start the process.
>
> Can you please get back to me regarding whether it's possible to start this course this academic year?

Many thanks

Shola Adewale Sandy

She replied back to me on the 6th of October 2008.

Shola

Yes, it is possible – we have had one session – You would need to attend either tomorrow or Tuesday 14th October

Please let me know

Regards

Deborah

I emailed her back on the same day requesting an application form, hoping I could get it all sorted quickly without missing any more sessions.

In order to be permitted an absence from school, several forms needed to be filled out, requiring details such as when and where the course was, and what days I would need off etc. The course was one day a week and it needed to be signed by Wendy, Grant and Charlotte. I filled in all the paperwork, got Wendy's signature and gave it to Grant plus the course details, so he and Charlotte could look over it and sign the relevant parts.

Grant approached me in the staffroom a few days later and said, "Charlotte said you cannot do the course."

I was a bit taken aback, and thought maybe he or she did not understand that I hadn't actually done the basic course that the job required since I started working in the school.

I asked, puzzled, "Why not?"

He had a blank expression and could not answer me and he gave me no eye contact. He went back downstairs, presumably to Charlotte.

He came back up to the staffroom, it could not have been more than ten minutes later, and said to me, "Other people are on this course already, that's why you cannot do it this year." (People that were employed after me, I later found out.)

I replied in a frustrated voice, "So when can I do it?"

He said, "Next year, if you book it on time."

I started to explain to him that it was actually affecting my wages, and why would I be employed for so long, without the relevant training that I had no choice, but to do? "So, I am doing a job, I am not trained to do?" – looking at him for an answer, some sort of explanation.

He then dropped a bombshell.

"If you really want to do the training, you need to apply for a Teaching Assistant job."

I looked at him in surprise and bewilderment, because I really didn't understand what he meant, applying for a Teaching Assistant job? Does that mean I would have to resign as a Cover Supervisor and look for a Teacher Assistant job for considerably less pay? Surely not!

Don't get me wrong, there was nothing wrong about being a TA, it's just that it was a completely different role to mine. They were not allowed to supervise a whole class alone and tended to work on a one-to-one basis with a student or a group, they had less workload and no other roles within the school. TAs are valuable members of staff as they are an extra hand, eyes and ears within the classroom, but nevertheless they were paid much less than a Cover Supervisor.

We were both standing, but I had to lean on a chair, because I could not believe what I was hearing from him. He was the one who interviewed me for this job and knew my job description. I said, "Why would I apply to be a TA, just to do the course?" Hoping he would think about what he was saying.

And he replied confidently, "You are really good at your job, that's why!"

I could not believe what I was hearing – what does he mean?

I said, "I would rather that it was reflected in my pay, I feel as if you are patronising me."

Grant just shrugged, and walked off. I stood there for a while, thinking what just happened? My respect for Grant at that point diminished even further – he was my line manager, he is supposed to know what training I need. Just because I am good at my job and managed without the training, does not mean I shouldn't do it, and moreover I needed the training to move on to scale 5, that was the only way. He had shown an attitude of not giving a damn about the fact I was clearly upset, and I did not know what to do.

Firstly, I emailed Deborah making up any excuse,

Hiya Deborah,

Tried to organise it all, but it seems TOO many staff are doing courses, so the school has said it would not be possible for me to attend this time.

Sorry to mess you about, do you have the same course starting in January? or later in the year, so I can book my place now.

Thanks again for all!

Regards

Shola

I was extremely upset, at the way I was treated; it felt as if I did not matter and having to send this email did not make me look very professional. Deborah replied to me on the same day to inform me that the course only runs once a year. I was gutted! Even if it did run later in the year, judging by Grant's comments and body language, it was clear he and Charlotte did not feel the need for me to attend.

BPAP

At this point BPAP was going from strength to strength, 40 plus boys at times. Debbie and I were running sessions straight after school until 6pm, we were exhausted, but it was so worth it, knowing the boys were safe with us. They really wanted somewhere they could go to after school that was informal and where they would not feel intimidated.

The climate at the time was *'Stop and Search'* by the police, the boys were angry about the way it was being enforced. At the time the school had a resident school liaison Police Officer named Brad, whom I mentioned before, remember, in the 'Dolton incident!'. He was helpful in many ways, as just being present at the school gates and within the school was a deterrent and some boys felt reassured about their safety.

Debbie and I wanted the sessions to be in a safe environment; we used the Pastoral Building from the start. It had a sink and a preparation area that we could prepare something hot and make snacks, sofas so the boys could relax, plus classrooms which could be used for *'break-out'* discussions. The objective of the sessions was to cover many issues such as increasing the boys' confidence, increasing their social skills, learning to interact with one another without being aggressive, respecting themselves, each other and the opposite sex.

We wanted them to have something hot to eat and drink which helped get them through the door and focused them on making a positive contribution. Other members of staff would help when they could; one of the regular helpers was Louise, a Citizenship Teacher – she came to the school through the *'Teach first'* pathway to becoming a teacher. She was super organised, but struggled initially with the behaviour of the boys. Coming to the sessions helped her improve her relationship with the boys, plus we really needed the extra help.

Initially, when we started Debbie and I served the snacks, it was like a mad rush that you would expect at an Ikea 90% off sale! We had to go back to bare basics and teach them to say "please and thank you" and to queue in an orderly fashion. I later learnt that those skills we were teaching them was called the '*The Hidden Curriculum*'. Slowly the boys learnt and started to take over our roles following a rota; it was amazing to see! They played table tennis, board games which we provided, and we had numerous discussions on relationships, sex, drugs, money, aspirations, personal hygiene and responsibility.

Birkbeck University

Ina, the talkative, but loveable HLTA had seen a Maths course by Birkbeck University advertised for adult learners. This course works around the older working person with other commitments like work or kids, with classes in the evening and on Saturdays.

Ina persuaded me to go for an open day event held in Stratford's Old Town hall with her, as we both had a passion for Maths. I spoke to a senior lecturer who was there from Birkbeck, he interestedly inquired about my background and then he informed me that I would have to come to the campus and sit a test to check out my subject knowledge. He also mentioned the financial cost of the course (which I nearly choked on!).

I had to go to the main campus just off Russell Square in Central London to find out more about the course and to do an initial test to make sure my maths was good enough to understand the topics to be taught; thankfully I passed. I took money from my meagre savings and paid for the course, close to a grand, but I thought it was a good opportunity to increase my subject knowledge and invest in myself.

The course was going to run in the main campus and parallel classes would be taking place in East London University – that swung it for me, it was right on my doorstep! Classes would be every Wednesday and Thursday from 6-9pm with some Saturday lectures at the main campus.

Thankfully starting the course at Birkbeck University allowed me to have something positive to focus on. Ina had got through the first stage, but dropped out at a later stage – the course was quite demanding with assignments and tests.

Our Thursday Further Maths lecturer was a man named Dr Loannis Kouletisis; he was so intense. I would go into his class and three hours would fly by. He made it so interesting, partial fractions, complex numbers, second order differential equations were some of the topics we tackled. I would end up with pages of notes; I felt elated, but mentally exhausted after his lectures.

I really was enjoying this course, as it was stimulating and I was treated equally by my peers. Nine times out of ten, I was late for class because the BPAP sessions had just finished before, and I would arrive humping and puffing, but the lecturers were really understanding, as many of the classes was made up of mature students with full time jobs.

One of them was Jenny aka 'Dreads' for her chosen hairstyle, she was a Maths teacher in a secondary school in Tower Hamlets. She was so calm and silently confident. I was in awe of her. Dreads was doing the course because she wanted to stimulate her brain and have more independent learning away from school, she had a passion for maths too, so we got on really well.

On one of our breaks, I confided in her about what was happening to me at Rokeby. Mainly, the difference in treatment between Daniel aka L and me. She was disgusted with what I was going through and asked me whether I had considered resigning. I told her what had happened to past employees.

Washeila had been an Information Technology teacher originally from South Africa. She had some issues which she brought to Ms Robinson's attention. It seemed the only way to resolve the matter was for her to leave immediately, was Ms Robinson's conclusion; she was not even allowed to say goodbye. I remember most of the staff met her at the local pub to say their farewells after school. What was really shocking is when Washeila requested a reference, to her disappointment, it was just seven lines, ironically one for each year she worked at Rokeby!

Another example of Ms Robinson's appalling behaviour was with Esther, her former PA, a shapely woman from Ghana; she had a likeable personality and was very efficient at her job. She was always dashing here and there, running errands for Ms Robinson. Esther was pregnant around the time I started and had returned from maternity

THURSDAY JUNE 11TH 2020

leave to find that her job had been taken up by another person and she had been moved to another room.

Esther was delegated to photocopying for a reason she did not understand. She was so taken aback by this and stressed out, she involved the union and eventually HR, but the summary of the advice given to her, was that if she was not happy with the change, she should leave.

On top of this she felt that the office staff were bullying her, as she had somewhat been demoted. Esther was really upset and did not know what to do, having two young children and the stress at Rokeby took its toll and she finally did resign, as she had run out of options to change her situation. The rest of the staff including me were shocked that this had happened so easily. I remember when Esther was on her maternity leave, coming into school with her baby boy, she had looked so happy and content but was eager to be returning to work soon.

Fast forward a few months and she looked like a broken woman, having to leave a place she had considered her second home. She had been such an efficient, hardworking individual, but none of that meant anything on her departure.

I was worried that Ms Robinson would do the same to me. If I was to apply for other Cover Supervisor roles, I would have to remain on scale 4 which would mean all my work for the last two years was pointless. I was dedicated to my work with the students at Rokeby, I didn't want to be another member of staff, who came and went, without a care in the world like many had done before. I was there for the duration, if only Charlotte aka Stone would allow me! The students behaved sometimes as if they don't want you there, but truly they did. Stability made them thrive, which ultimately is the main objective.

Dreads enjoyed where she was working and really didn't understand why I was going through all of my drama. She was one of the first people to encourage me to become a qualified Maths teacher.

"Shola, how did you work that out? I like your method better."

"Thanks," I replied, obviously embarrassed, but thrilled hearing that from her.

"You would be a really good Maths Teacher, Shola; I can see you got skills!" I thought that was so funny, if only I could do that. Imagine going to school every day and teaching the subject you love and getting paid for it, can you imagine??

She gave me so much confidence in the subject itself and talked to me about other tasks that a teacher had to do, like writing schemes of work, understanding data, preparing assessments and marking books. She wanted to let me know it wasn't just about 'standing in front of a class' and spilling out information.

I needed a distraction from all the madness that was going on at work. We would work together in East London University's library on assignments and test each other on the various topics we were doing. If it wasn't for her, I don't know how I would have completed the course. It was also good to be able to chat to Dreads about what was going on at school and get her independent opinion.

Of course, she said it was not fair the way I was being treated and couldn't understand why I was not getting the support I needed to develop within the school.

I loved sitting down along with my peers and learning, it was so empowering. I didn't mind the 6pm classes at East London University campus coming straight from work, because I knew my brain was being nourished. At the end of class, normally 9pm, I would be mentally and physically drained but exhilarated that I had manged to attend another lesson, leaving with my sprits high, walking into the chilled dark nights.

Friday June 12th, 2020

This was the evening where another black man's life was taken. Excessive force in my opinion and it was all caught on CCTV. Thankfully, for the world to see again, so it could never be denied.

Rayshard Brookes, a 27-year-old with three daughters, was parked up at a Wendy's drive-through in Atlanta in the States. There was so much video footage from various cameras, so we were not totally sure of the sequences of events that led up to this black man's unfortunate, but predictable end.

All I could see was that the police tried to arrest him when he failed a field sobriety test. There was a struggle and he managed to get away with a Taser that belonged to one of the officers. He started running and was more than five cars away, when he turned, most probably in fear and attempted to shoot the Taser at one of the chasing officers. That police officer, now known as Garrett Rolfe, shot Rayshard three times in the back; he was sacked soon after the event and his partner in crime, Devin Bronsan, was put on administrative duties.

***

Other training

I started looking for some other training at school, as it seemed I was not allowed on the Teaching Assistant course. One of the programmes that caught my attention was the Graduate Teaching Programme (GTP), it was designed for anyone who had a degree and wanted to become a teacher. It was based in the school setting, in the sense that you would have a certain amount of classes you would have to teach. You would be constantly observed by a chosen mentor in the school and your progress reviewed regularly. Some written projects were required, plus attending some university sessions, where you would be able to meet other students on the GTP, network and exchange ideas. The programme could be completed in six months to a year, depending on the applicant's experience and progress.

The most important aspect of this programme is that you get into a school that will provide you with a mentor and classes for you to teach. There is no guarantee that the school would employ you at the end of your training, but if a vacancy came up, then your chances were as good as any other candidate. Some schools may prefer you over anyone else as you have already worked with the students in the school.

GTP in Maths would have been fantastic for me!

I knew the school would not be out of pocket, as the funding attached to this programme was more than sufficient. Liz, one of the science HLTAs had been on the programme, but not completed it. Also a Spanish language teacher, Helena, had just completed the training, but was unsuccessful in applying for a vacant post at the school.

There were other ways to apply for teacher training. The most popular options were Post Graduate Certificate in Education (PGCE) – this was for degree holders again and it required you to work in two schools with lectures and assignments over a period of a year.

Teach First were for high calibre individuals recruited from the financial district in the City with first class degrees, preferably coming from an ethnic minority. This was the pathway that Louise, the Citizenship teacher, had taken. She was working previously in the

City as a lawyer and came from a Caribbean background. It was an intense programme over the summer, with you starting a role in the September with immense support. If you could get through that, then it was likely you would move up the ranks quite fast with a leadership position, once you completed the probationary period. This is what attracted the candidates, plus making a difference to students in inner city schools.

I spoke to Grant Leppard to ok it with him, and he directed me to Mick, who said that it was a good idea, but he said he might not be able to be my mentor, as he was busy with other roles. Mick told me to approach Grant Bulmuo aka 'Pastor', who was the Head of the Maths Department. He really was a 'real life' working Pastor with a loyal congregation.

Anyway, I had covered his lessons many times, he had always been satisfied and in some cases impressed with the work I did, and I heard that he had gone through the same programme, so I thought he would be able to relate.

I felt comfortable enough to speak to Pastor, I explained to him about my situation, I said I had run it past Grant and Mick already, and I asked him whether he would support me if I applied for the GTP. I couldn't think of a reason why he wouldn't do it.

"You have said in the past I would be a good teacher; here is a programme I can do within the school to become qualified."

It had my name all over it. I handed him the paperwork, and he said he would be more than happy to support me. I started to get excited.

"I will look into it, Shola but would have to agree it with Charlotte in any case."

I thought, I wouldn't have to go on this damn TA course and my pay would rise substantially, plus the school would get some allowance, so it's a win-win for all. I could not see any reason why Charlotte would not agree to it.

I didn't want to hassle him to speed it along. "Any news?" I would ask Pastor periodically about whether I could start with the paperwork, but he kept fobbing me off. Eventually, he said that he had bought it up in a SLT meeting.

"Charlotte has said no, you can't do the course."

I was so confused – had he explained the course to her properly?

"Why ever not?" I managed to get out.

"She just said no, the school doesn't do it anymore."

I was taken aback, as Helena in the language department had just completed the programme.

There was nothing I could do, I was so disappointed, but I had to just accept the answer and continue to do my job as best as I could.

***

During this time, unfortunately: Jo walker had moved to another school, Mick Eryes had left and Pastor had been promoted.

I could not just leave it there regarding the GTP, this was my chance!

I thought if I met up with Charlotte aka Stone to get my point across, maybe she would understand my situation, even though I knew she despised me. I felt reassured that as a Head teacher she would have to be professional and treat me equally and allow me to have some form of career development like Daniel and the other members of staff. I tried to meet up with her on several occasions, but she was always too busy; she finally found a slot for me at 7.00am on the 12th of December 2008.

On the day, I was in school at 6.30am. Excited to get my point across to Stone – surely she would understand the need for me to be on this course, regardless of how she felt about me. I went to the staffroom to make myself a hot drink, Debbie was in as usual getting ready for breakfast club. I chatted with her for a while and headed

FRIDAY JUNE 12TH, 2020

down to Stone's office around 6.55am. Her office was quite big, with comfy chairs and a large table at the far end.

She was sitting there and motioned me to sit down in front of the table. It felt like a job interview with her towering over me. It was a frosty atmosphere; I could tell she would rather be anywhere else than sitting here with me.

I initially asked her about the GTP, and she said the school did everything else like Teach First and PGCE, but not the GTP, because there was too much paperwork, also there were no posts vacant. I thought to myself, that's not strictly true, Ms Robinson, Mick Eyres has just left and sadly Jo Walker too, so there were classes available. Agencies had been filling in, costing the school a small fortune; either way, I didn't want to push the matter too much further, and she was not budging.

Trying another angle. I replied, "I have not had any career development, this would be really good for me and my well-being. Even though you are saying, the school doesn't do it now, there have been teachers, since I have been at this school, that have gone through it." I was thinking of Helena, who had just completed the training and obviously Liz the science HLTA.

She replied, "We do not do it anymore and will not be doing it, but other schools in Newham do."

I thought why is she is saying this about other schools? I am obviously only concerned with this school, as this is where I work. One of the hardest requirements of the GTP is to have a school and a mentor; I had both.

I said, "I don't want to leave, Charlotte. Would the school make an exception for me, as I have received no training, this would be an ideal way forward for me." One last push, I thought.

She repeated exasperatedly, "The school will not be offering that programme."

I had to let it go, what more could I say? So, I said reservedly, "If that's the case, is there any other relevant training I could do?"

"I will speak to Grant about that, and he will get back to you."

I sighed, feeling defeated, and moved on to my pay.

"Is there any way to increase my salary, because I am doing a lot around the school, and it is not reflected in my wages. You have the discretion to move me to scale 5, it would make such a difference to me!" Surely, on this point, she would understand.

She replied, "Will speak to Shelley about that, and she will get back to you." She shuffled in her chair.

I realized that was my cue to leave, I thanked her for her time and left.

I felt deflated after the meeting and was not holding my breath for any change to her decision. I thought to myself why was she willing to approve all this work I was doing around the school, but not willing to support me to get the relevant training and the pay that came with it?

Moving on to scale 5 would mean my pay would go up incrementally yearly until I reached the top of scale 5 – why did she not want to give me that opportunity? I was simply insignificant to her; she clearly was not interested in my predicament.

I did get an email from Shelley six days later to say that my wages would not increase until I had completed the course, surprise surprise!

Grant aka Useless did put a booklet in my pigeonhole. I initially thought it was put there by mistake, but saw a single, yellow post it note attached to it, with my name on it. I looked through the booklet but all the courses were not relevant to me and most importantly would not get me on to scale 5. I thought to myself, is Grant taking the mick out of me? I had an image of him chuckling to himself in his office at me, while I flipped through the useless booklet.

Ho Ho Ho!

I remembered an incident that had happened at the end of term around Christmas. About 15 members of staff including me were having a drink in the local pub. We were all around a big table chit-chatting and enjoying the evening. I was sitting next to a fairly new member of staff.

Ms Higgins taught humanities and I was inquiring how she was finding working at the school. Out of nowhere she brought the email incident up; she asked whether the rumour was true.

"Are you the schools drug dealer?" She obviously was joking because she chuckled. I instantly looked around because I was not sure whether anyone had overheard Ms Higgins, and wondered who had informed her of the email. I was embarrassed and shocked; if I could have turned beetroot red I would have. A thin film of sweat covered my whole body! I quickly tried to change the topic, which I managed to do.

I couldn't believe it!

This was more than a year after the email was sent. After a respectable few minutes, I made my apologies and left the pub. I was still dealing with the after-effects of Shelley's email; I just wanted it to go away permanently, but it just kept coming back to haunt me.

And just to put the cherry on the cake, Grant aka Useless had approached me and said I was now part of the Humanities Department. I was sceptical about his sudden change of heart, no discussion just an order. I would have preferred being linked to the Maths department, but I would make it work in Humanities. At least finally I would get to:

- *Go on training or Career development linked to the subject.*
- *Integrate into the Department and be part of a team, e.g. meetings, inset days.*
- *Go on organised trips, attend parent evenings.*

- *Be informed of the curriculum for the year, which would also help me in my cover supervising role.*
- *Be linked to Key Stage 3 (years 7, 8 and 9) or Key Stage 4 (years 10 and 11).*

He then went on to say that the Humanities department had a lot of staff, and because they did not have any technicians or a secretary, I was to bridge that gap. My grand plans fell down like dominos in a flash. I was obviously disappointed, and expressed this to Grant, but I didn't want to sound ungrateful. Over the next few months, I remained hopeful, that I would be doing something interesting and fulfilling, but nothing ever materialised.

Ms Higgins was the Head of Humanities, and after our exchange in the pub, she was frosty towards me, which didn't bother me too much. It was when she started to demand photocopying within the hour or to call parents pronto, putting notes in my pigeonhole, not taking into account that I was covering lessons. When I asked Grant aka Useless to have a word with her, that didn't work, so I had to put it bluntly to her. I knew they were taking advantage of me and my hard working nature, but I didn't know what else to do.

I was the best photocopier the world had ever seen, and would organise whatever I had to photocopy neatly for the department in their pigeonholes or on their desks. I had to do the things required of me from the Humanities Department whenever I could, on top of all my other duties.

But when I attempted to attend departmental meetings, I was told by Ms Higgins with a sarcastic smile, it was not necessary for me to attend, I really took it to heart…

Hair loss

By this time, I had started to lose my hair in clumps, I didn't know why this was happening. Initially I tried to hide it, like how some balding men swipe the only lock of hair across their forehead to hide the obvious space, I did the same and would cover the bald patches with the hair I had left. Hubby advised me to go to the doctor, just to check it out. I personally thought maybe I was going through the menopause early, especially as I was still only in my 30s!

After the doctor examined my scalp and ordered a blood test, he said, "How are you sleeping?"

"Not very well, Doc," I replied.

"Is there anything going on in your life that's occupying your thoughts?"

Immediately I thought of the elephant in the room!

"I feel quite stressed with work." I tried to keep it simple

"Well, stress can cause your hair to fall out. You need to find a way to deal with it and reduce your stress levels." Easier said than done, Doc – how on earth was I going to do that?

Signing in issue

Back in November 2008, I started getting emails, regarding a signing in/out procedure from Shelley, which she wanted to implement straightaway. I thought initially that it was a mistake, as nothing was said in briefing, I had never signed in or out ever since I started the job, and no-one had discussed it with me. I had not heard anything from anyone from SLT and I really did not know what she was on about.

My first reaction was why is she still one of my managers? She had never managed me. If I had a say in the matter, after the email incident she should not have been allowed to manage me at all. Debbie was also getting emails regarding the same thing. Debbie's concern was that she was in school before everyone else and she was not going to interrupt her important work with the students to go to the office and sign in. She left the school around 5 or 6pm every day; by then it was past the office closing time of 4.30pm. It was such a strange request because Shelley knew the apparent book to sign in was in the locked reception office which opened at 8.30am and closed at 4.30pm.

I too would arrive early and leave late on most days. I could not see how this would be implemented, and I was extremely worried about any repercussions. For example, if I forgot to sign in or out occasionally, what would happen? It might have been a dramatic way to think, but nevertheless I wanted some sort of explanation or meeting to clarify why was this being implemented and what the process involved and finally any repercussions, like I said before.

Cherelle, the other Cover Supervisor, did not want any trouble. She just started signing in and out without asking any questions. Cherelle was recently new and did not have any tasks in the morning and left soon after school finished to pick up her child. She came in minutes before she had to sign in in the mornings. I, on the other hand, was out at the gate by that time or occupied with other tasks. I wanted to know beforehand all the details, so I would not get into trouble. I didn't want to be hauled into any disciplinary meetings.

Already Charlotte aka Stone would often go looking for Cherelle in classrooms while she was covering lessons, and ask her why she had forgotten to sign-in, right in front of the students. She would stand around and remind her to do so at her earliest convenience. Cherelle was getting quite stressed at this point. I thought this was strange for the Head teacher to be doing this, hence why I wanted these questions answered; I didn't think I was being unreasonable.

In the mornings around that time, Debbie could be finishing breakfast club or visiting students at home to give them missed work or even taking students to the Stratford shopping centre to replace shoes that were leaking or torn. It would be done in a discreet manner

FRIDAY JUNE 12TH, 2020

because some parents could not afford it and were too proud to ask for it. The students themselves would cringe if their peers knew their business. It would amaze me what lengths she went to, to make sure the students had a chance and stayed in school; even if they ended up in prison, she would encourage them to stay strong and focus on the positives from there.

Debbie has been abused verbally so much with the most vulgar words by some of the past and present students, but it usually went right over her head. She had been threatened and physically lashed out at, but she would calmly deal with the situation, communicating with the parents or carers, trying to work together to find a way forward.

She dealt with social services, police, homeless agencies, prison service, just to mention a few. I learnt so much from her, she taught me to look beyond the behaviour and start each day as a fresh beginning with each student.

Debbie taught the students to have self-worth and respect for themselves and believe they too could have a bright future. Now she has to remember to sign in and if she forgets all hell would break loose and management would come after her.

I mentioned the signing in issue several times over those months to Grant aka Useless. I would ask him, "Why was this being implemented now?" He replied, "It's part of your contract." I asked him about the repercussions and the location of the signing in book, but he just shrugged. So frustrating!

On reflection, I thought maybe it would be a good idea if EVERYONE signed in especially as sometimes teachers were out of school, but no-one would be aware until the school was in full swing. I had first-hand experience of this when my rota was changed numerous times to accommodate the sudden absences, typically just before the bell goes for the first lesson!

Even though I particularly did not want to meet with Shelley – the thought of it made me feel like throwing up – I thought that this would be the best way to iron out the issues I had, or at least have a dialogue or some sort of discussion about this damn signing in/out thing!

I asked Grant aka Useless to help me arrange it, as he would always answer my questions with perplexed looks of puzzlement. I knew that he had talked to her because I received a letter at the end of January from Shelley attempting to address the issues I had raised with Grant. Why could she not just sit down with me and discuss it like a normal human being?

She stated that the reason this procedure was to be implemented was for the health and safety of only the support staff. Two incidents were mentioned: one staff member could not be contacted, and the second: confusion surrounding a staff member who might or might not have informed the school of his/her absence.

She said Debbie and I were the only members of staff not doing it. Finally, she concluded that she had got advice from the *Head of School Services* and the *Health and Safety Officer of Schools* and both had apparently said that it was not an unreasonable request, so in conclusion we were to start signing in from the 9th of February as requested.

It was clear that I was becoming more unwell due to this situation and everything else happening at the school. I was not sleeping well – waking up after a few hours, thinking about my situation. My immune system was very low, so I kept getting colds, coughs and feeling genuinely unwell.

Around this time my hair continued to fall out in the back and middle, I had so many bald patches, I had to start wearing a wig, because my beautiful hair was not presentable anymore.

I put this down to the fact that I was under a lot of stress from Charlotte, Grant and Shelley. My simple questions were not being answered and I felt I was being harassed and bullied into doing something that did not make any sense at all. I expressed this clearly to Shelley in a letter on the 4th of February.

FRIDAY JUNE 12TH, 2020

Dear Shelley,

In response to your letter, regarding the signing in/out book, I agree with your reasons for having a signing in book. I also agree it is not un-reasonable to ask me to sign it. What I find difficult to understand is why don't all staff sign it, especially the teachers?

There have been numerous occasions at the start of the period or even registration, staff cannot be found (examples can be given if requested) and I have had to undertake their tasks, or rearrange my schedule, only to find out later that the member of staff is not even in school, or is in school, but nobody was aware of their presence. If this issue did not affect me personally, I would not have an opinion on the matter and for those who do sign in, it's their choice.

I have never been absent and not informed the school and as far as I am aware, covered all my required classes. From what you have said previously ALL staff will be signing in /out at the new school, so why not now? As it is in the interest of ALL staff working in the school.

Surely the health and safety of ALL staff is important now and not just at the new school?

I will be quite happy to sign it, once my queries have been answered satisfactorily, can you please get back to me regarding this issue, as it is causing me immense stress and is not allowing me to focus on the job I am employed to do.

Yours sincerely, Shola Adewale Sandy

She emailed me back re-iterating what she had said in her first letter, saying it should not be a matter that should cause me immense stress, and I should just do it. Can you imagine?!

This woman is asking me to walk into a lion's trap with my eyes open! I was damned if I did it, as I was sure Charlotte aka Stone would have started chasing me up like she did with Cherelle, and if I didn't, I would be facing disciplinary action for sure. I chose the latter option and so did Debbie as we felt so strongly about the issue.

On the 9th of February 2009, Shelley wrote to Debbie and me to inform us that we had not signed in that morning; she quoted a line from the Newham disciplinary rules and asked us to sign in. We continued not to sign in and received another letter to inform us that she would be carrying out an investigation on the 2nd of March, and we had the right to be accompanied by a trade union representative or friend.

I tried not to think about the upcoming signing in/out meeting with Shelley too much. The day was fast approaching. Debbie and I decided to get Unison involved by having someone present at the investigation. We went to the Unison office, which was based in a temporary caravan-like structure, besides East Ham town hall on the Barking Road.

Jay, the union rep, put us at ease straight away. He could see that we were both concerned about our jobs and the implications this signing in/out would present. He reassured us in a calm manner that he would do some research on the issue, and would be attending the investigation meetings with us.

On the 2nd of March, Jay arrived at the school on a bike with all the safety clothing that went with it. Debbie and I looked at each other doubtfully, hoping he knew the importance of the meeting. Jay quickly secured his bike, and took off the bike gear, leaving him looking rather smart. We were both nervous, but after a few moments chatting with him, we felt reassured and confident as we waited in the foyer to be called into the office, where the meeting was taking place.

FRIDAY JUNE 12TH, 2020

Debbie was looking sharp as usual, she had "power dressed" for the occasion, her long fingernails were painted a fiery red, and she had on bright red, shiny heels, she wore a fitted top and skirt, and her hair was slicked back into a ponytail. I on the other hand was wearing black trousers and a dark top, with black flat shoes. I looked down at my outfit and wished I had made more of an effort. We were both tired, it had been a long school day, and I still had things to do, like incident reports and checking my emails. We were far from happy that we had to attend this formal investigation meeting and could not wait for it to be over. Debbie and I were to have separate meetings with Shelley.

My meeting was first. When I entered the room and saw Shelley, my feelings of the email incident all came back in a rush and I felt slightly dizzy. I composed myself and sat down quickly around the table. On the other side Denise, Charlotte's new PA, was getting ready to take the minutes. Shelley looked very confident and shuffled the heap of paperwork in front of her. I thought, that must be the health and safety rules that she had quoted in her letters and most probably the school's disciplinary procedures. I took a big gulp and looked over at Jay, thank God he was here, but you could see that Shelley was slightly taken aback that Jay was present.

After the introductions, Shelley began the meeting, by saying this meeting was about my refusal to follow a management request to sign in/out on a daily basis, she recapped what had happened, most likely for the benefit of Jay. She said she had asked me to sign in several times and so had Grant aka Useless. She then turned to me and asked why had I not done so.

I took a deep breath in and replied, "As outlined in my letter to you, we never had any discussion or meeting as to what and why, all I got were emails, more importantly if all staff are not included, what is the point of the signing in book? When staff are absent, this affects me as I do cover, none of my questions have been answered!" I just spilled out all my concerns on the table one time.

Shelley replied, "Apologises, with hindsight a meeting could have been arranged to discuss details, but the reasons why members of support staff were asked to sign is that they are all contracted to work different hours."

I said in frustration, "I don't understand why we ALL can't sign in?"

Jay saw me getting worked up and said to Shelley, "Can I get clarity. Do teachers have to come in at a specific time and is signing in/out a Health and Safety issue?"

Shelley replied, "At a meeting with other Newham Bursars I asked if this was acceptable and I have also spoken to Trevor Matthews."

I hastily said, "I spoke to Trevor Matthews too and he told me to refer back to the union."

Debbie and I had called him, when we had received Shelley's letter, and he had said quite clearly that when a new procedure is introduced, the staff affected should be consulted with the assistance of the union, so any issues would be ironed out at that stage.

Jay directed a question at Shelley: "There is no policy then?"

I quickly said, "I am not happy with signing in if it's not a Health and Safety issue, it is making me stressed and stopping me from doing my job properly." I had to voice this, as I really did not see the point of this procedure.

Shelley said, "I did not want you to feel stressed."

I thought to myself, for someone who sits in her office creating procedures and emailing her husband, she has no idea what I am going through. She had no direct contact with the students, so she couldn't possibly comment on my stress levels.

I said, "This is not being dealt with in the right way, I feel victimised and bullied." I thought it's the way she has gone about trying to implement it. Ever since the email incident, any opportunity to put me in a corner or speak to me in a disrespectful manner, she took.

There was a pause and then Jay said, "If this is not a Health & Safety issue, why do support staff have to sign in?"

Shelley said, "Because support staff have different start and finish times."

Jay said, "Has a Health & Safety risk assessment been done?"

Shelley replied hesitantly, "No."

He was quite surprised by that and said, "Shola and I have had a conversation. What I hope would happen is if we are unable to find a solution because of the way the signing in issue was implemented, in hindsight could it have been done differently, is it a tool to locate staff? Is a sickness procedure in place?"

Shelley replied "Yes" to the last question.

Jay said, "Because no conversation and no meeting took place, it makes the situation difficult to understand. I have spoken to Alan Merry. There is no mandate in the Borough, I am unsure as to why you are asking staff to sign in when you have not provided an explanation. Why are staff being asked to sign in?"

Shelley tried to reply but started to stumble over her words. It soon became clear with the questions that Jay was asking her that she was beginning to feel uncomfortable. "I have clearly stated the reasons why."

Jay said, "If it is no longer a Health & Safety issue what difference does it make, someone signing in a book?"

Shelley replied, "If needed, to check if staff are at work."

Jay said, "I think the problem here is lack of communication and people signing in is not going to help you find them. I don't think we shall get an agreement today. Can I ask is this a formal investigation?"

Shelley replied, "Yes."

Jay said, "I think that by not all staff signing in, is that not discriminatory? Today it is not a Health & Safety issue, before it was a Health & Safety issue, by not asking teachers to sign in, is their Health & Safety not being managed?"

Shelley said, "The nature of support staff work is that they are all doing different things, not structured time, some work by themselves, some work in two different departments. If they sign-in, we know they are in school."

I mumbled, all I ever wanted was an explanation as to why this new procedure had to be introduced immediately, why couldn't the people involved not following the rules, be spoken to individually? If I was not in school for whatever reason, I always followed the right procedure and contacted the school to let them know.

Jay said, "We are no closer to getting clarity."

I piped up and said, "At the new school we will all have to swipe in and out, why can't we all sign in and out now? If I was asked to swipe in/out at the new school I would, because everyone will be doing it."

Jay directed a question at Shelley: "Why do teachers not have to sign in?"

Shelley replied, "They work to different contracts under directed time."

Jay then said, "But they could be asked?"

Shelley replied, "I am not in charge of teachers."

Jay then said, "Who is, the head teacher?"

Shelley said, "Yes, they have to be in by 8.15am."

Jay said, "All staff have to ring in by 8.15am?"

Shelley said, "We have procedures in place for all staff."

Jay said, "Teachers have to phone in sick by 7.30am but there have been occurrences where they have not phoned by 7.30 and Shola has not been informed – good reason for teachers to sign in." Jay then addressed me. "I think we have four choices:

Sign in

Don't sign in

Continue not to sign in and face conduct disciplinary action

Remove signing in book" – he directed this to Shelley.

Jay then said to Shelley, "Because there was no presentation initially to support staff, now to ask them how they feel about signing in is strange."

Shelley said reluctantly, "We aim to find a resolution," but stated she would not be rushed into making any decisions.

It was apparent from the meeting, that the signing in/out issue had to be implemented for all staff or none at all. I was embarrassed for her for not doing all her research, trying to implement a procedure without any consultation. You could see she wanted the floor to just cave in and swallow her up. She became that innocent child-like person, who when no one was looking was plotting the most hideous things. I was not buying it, especially as I had seen this scene before. I thought she was going to start crying to complete the effect, but thankfully she didn't.

Debbie's meeting was straight after, and was a repeat of mine, except this time when Jay asked Shelley questions, her head was down. After a while she stopped answering questions, just sat there and remained silent. Debbie was surprised with Shelley's demeanour – after all, she had been the one sending letters and emails to us for the past few months stressing us out, and when she was put on the spot, she could not defend or give an adequate explanation to this procedure she wanted to implement.

We both could not believe the outcome, we were so impressed with the way Jay handled the meetings, he was calm throughout and pointed out the obvious; when he spoke, the content was precise and fair. After this meeting I encouraged Cherelle to become a member, just in case the need for support arises at her time at Rokeby, just like Seamus had advised me months before.

Debbie and I continued not to sign in, waiting in anticipation for Shelley's response. We expected to be told every member of staff had to start signing in/out, even though we didn't know how in practice it would work. I overheard a teacher saying, "If we have to start signing in and out, I will just get someone else to do it for me!" and laughed. I thought to myself, they did have a point.

Finally, after a few days, we both received a letter from Shelley in our pigeonholes. I hurriedly opened mine and read the following:

Dear Shola

Re: Signing in and out

This is to inform you that no further action will be taken regarding the investigation into the above matter.

Yours sincerely

Shelley

I could not believe it! One line! What does it mean? Is the signing in/out book being banished to the cellar or not? Do I or don't I have to sign in? Debbie's letter was the same. Both of us would have liked to have had some sort of an apology or a statement to say, if there is going to be any change in procedure in the future, the relevant people need to be involved in the process, but we got neither.

***

After the 'signing in/out' issue, Debbie was going on a training course, and she wanted me to cover her lunch duty, which I had no problem doing.

She cleared it with her line manager at the time, Gurgit Shergill, who arranged for someone to be at my post in the playground. When I got into the dining hall, I spoke to Grant aka Useless, who said that would be ok.

FRIDAY JUNE 12TH, 2020

I proceeded to do the shift, and about three-quarters of the way through, Charlotte aka Stone comes upstairs into the dining hall. She did not speak to me, which I was used to by now, she walked around the dining hall and spoke to Grant and left five minutes later.

Once my duty was over, I went to Period 5, but about 30 minutes into the lesson, I got a message that Grant wanted to see me straight after school in his office.

I was concerned, and could not focus properly on the rest of my lesson. I did not know what it was about and I do not recall having a positive meeting with Grant since he had become my direct line manager after Mick had left the school.

I walked into the meeting, and he said, "A bit of bad news, I am afraid, I know you always seem to be getting bad news!"

I replied, "Ok." I took a deep breath and sat down.

Grant proceeded to say, "Charlotte wanted to know, why you were in the dining hall? She was not happy that you were not at your post in the playground."

I just looked at him; I did not know what to say as it was quite obvious why I was there: why didn't he tell her, I was covering for Debbie?

Debbie had followed procedure and informed the right people. If Charlotte aka Stone had asked me why I was there, while walking round the dining hall, then the whole situation would not have been blown out of proportion and I would not have been summoned for a pointless meeting.

Anyway, after this incident, can you imagine, Grant sent me a new rota for lunch duty. I was placed in the dining hall two days a week and three days outside; Lord give me strength!

I had done lunch duty in the dining hall previously and had been dismissed from that duty abruptly by Charlotte aka Stone for no apparent reason. I wrote to him to put me somewhere else, but he replied that that was not possible, because it had been discussed and agreed by the Senior Leadership Team.

Just to mention, the Senior Leadership Team do not teach full time, so are supposed to, in theory, do break/lunch and gate duty. Last count, there must have been up to 15 in the team: Heads of Year, Key Stage Coordinators, Heads of Departments, other people with responsibility etc.

I should only in theory be doing these duties occasionally, not every single day! I was getting tired of being shoved from one post to another, without any thought about my cover work and all the other roles I was doing within the school. On top of the fact that I was still not getting the proper wage that was advertised for the role I was doing.

Saturday June 13th, 2020

The far-right protesters had gone down to protect the Churchill statue, even though it was boarded up top to toe already. They had banners saying:

"All lives matter" and surrounded the boarded-up statue. It seemed they were drinking and it looked like they wanted to fight the police, telling the officers aggressively and egging them on: "Take a knee, go on take the knee!" You could see the venom in their faces and foam spurting out from their mouths, as hardly any face masks were visible. What vile behaviour!

The Black Lives Matter protesters had planned to march in the area, as they have been doing for the last few weeks. It had been hyped up all week and certain black community leaders, parents and even grandparents wanted to be present to oversee any wrong moves by the far-right protesters.

Once the two groups of protesters met, it got ugly, as missiles, punches and verbal abuse were thrown. A white protester from the 'far right group' was injured and in harm's way – I was proud to see a strong well-built black man, not thinking of his own safety, swooped in, with the guidance of his friends and carried this *'fool'* out of harm's way. That image was caught on camera and circulated, before you could say 'Casablanca' it had gone viral all around the world!

Back to school

This is long winded, but bear with me. On the 24th of March, I was covering a science lesson. This practical room had two doors of entry, as well as a fire door to the car park. After ten minutes into the lesson, a boy named Michael appears; apparently, he had been locked in the loo. Michael was a Year 7 student, with a very troubled background; I had spoken to other members of staff about him before, as he was a cause for concern.

He was a nice enough boy, but extremely streetwise. He reminded me of the Artful Dodger, complete with the oversized clothes and permanent dirt on his face and under his fingernails. He came in and started playing about under the table. I sent him out and called for 'on-call'; in the meantime, he kept banging on each of the doors and opening and closing them. There was nothing I could do, but reprimand him and focus on the rest of the good behaviour of the other students. I hoped he would not dash into the class and out the fire door – the students were becoming distracted from doing their tasks with him making so much noise.

Eventually, when no 'on-call' arrived, I made the executive decision to end the lesson a few minutes before the bell went. My intentions were to walk them to the gate as it was the end of the day, but as I came out of the class Charlotte aka Stone was there. She did not look or speak to me, she just told the boys to go back into the room, as the bell had not gone yet. I was puzzled by this as she did not inquire why I had called 'on-call' or why I had let the boys out.

As they turned to come back into the room the bell went, so they immediately turned back around and made their way to the gate. By this time, Michael had scampered off as soon as he caught sight of Charlotte. I wrote an incident report, copying in Grant aka Useless and someone from the SEN department, and didn't give the incident any more thought.

Anyway, I received the following email:

SATURDAY JUNE 13TH, 2020

Shola

Following on from my two recent announcements in briefing instructing staff not to allow students to leave lessons before the bell (especially period 4) I was disappointed to meet several media studies students from your cover class at the dining room door, at approx. 12.53 today.

This is not the first time that I have had to speak to you about this matter. On Tuesday 24th March you let a year 7 science class out early – I was in the corridor and asked them to return to their classroom. I then spoke to you and asked that you do not release students before the bell.

When children are released early it puts unnecessary pressure on other staff.

A copy of this memo will go into your file.

Charlotte Robinson

I was very distressed, when I read this letter, to me it was the worst thing that could happen. I did not know anything about any Media students, this was the first time I was hearing about it. She also lied about speaking to me on the day of the incident with the Year 7 class. She had twisted the facts to make me look incompetent. I prided myself on doing my job well, and the fact that it was going into my file, I just could not be consoled, not even by Debbie!

She said, trying to console me, "This is no coincidence, Charlotte seems to be going for you!"

There was no discussion.

I could not believe that a Head teacher would write such things without investigating such matters. After hardly getting any sleep, I had no choice but to reply to her letter, and hopefully get the names of the Media students to get to the bottom of the matter.

After working in the school for this amount of time, without any issues to my quality of work and now all of this!

3rd April 2009

In regards to the memo dated 2nd April 2009

Dear Charlotte

Thank you for bringing to my attention that students from Mr O Brien's media class, I was covering went to lunch at 12.53pm.

I took the second part of a double lesson, and a few of the boys were trying to finish coursework that was due in at 1pm.

I was not aware that any boys went to lunch as I did not give them permission to do this.

They could either have:

1) Been working in another classroom during the first period.

2) Slipped out of the class when I was helping a student (the door remains open during lessons because of the heat generated by 25+ students and the numerous computers).

3) Or just skipping class.

I would like to know who the students are so the reasons for them being at lunch without my permission can be explained.

On the 24th March, I called "on-call" (see enclosed incident sheet) which I rarely do. The science class I was covering was getting out of control due to one student, hence the reason for calling "on-call".

To my understanding "on-call" is for emergencies, how can you continue a disruptive class, when you don't have any back up to deal with such situations?

After 25 minutes I had to deal with M.V and send the other students three minutes early as I could NOT continue the class with him banging/kicking/opening/closing the two science doors. On that particular day, you actually walked straight past me, without saying a word into the opposite room (23?) after sending the students back to class.

It's a shame that you feel disappointed with those two issues, in both cases instant verbal communication would have shed light on the situation, I FEEL it's a shame that was not done.

Hopefully this situation should not occur again, if it does can you communicate with me, before assuming the student's version of the situation is truthful.

Shola Adewale Sandy

I dropped the letter with Charlotte's PA early in the morning, hoping Charlotte aka Stone would see my point of view and arrange to have a meeting with me during the day to clear up the matter and hopefully take this off my file.

What was ironic was that during Period 1 of that day while I was covering Grant Bulmuo's lesson aka 'Pastor', Gurgit, Debbie's line manager, came into my class to bring some students back to the lesson.

She did not ask me whether the students were from this class, she just assumed that they were and I did not say anything. Gurgit was so convinced that the students belonged there, so it would not have mattered either way.

As it turns out, THOSE STUDENTS were not from my class. I found out when the register arrived and I had to send them back to their appropriate class which was, guess who? Yes, Charlotte's lesson, who did not realise she was missing some students! Can you imagine? Should I now put that in her file?

On the same day, Period 2, I sent a student outside the classroom as he was being disruptive, and had been giving me excuses about why he could not behave in the lesson. After I had settled the class, I went outside to talk to him to find out why he was behaving that way. To my surprise, when I got outside Charlotte was standing right there talking to him and looking into the class for no apparent reason. I thought," Maybe she wants to talk to me about the letter?", but she said nothing to me and walked away.

The same day, Period 3, I had just finished Break duty by the front gate, and was going to my next class. As I approached Room 9 in the Maths department, Charlotte aka Stone again was standing there for no obvious reason. This time she spoke. "You are late, didn't you know what class to go to?"

I was surprised and thought why is she reprimanding me in front of the students and why is she being so sarcastic? I have just finished doing break duty, after years of working at the school, I should know how to find my way around by now. I simply replied, "I am here now", and attempted to walk into the class. The students were surrounding us and wanted to go in too, I was embarrassed that she had talked to me in that tone of voice in front of the students. Some of them were looking at her puzzled – why was she just standing there?

It had been an eventful day and I really was on edge, not knowing who would be behind me, if I suddenly turned around. It was like having my own personal fleet of security guards that I was trying to shake off. This was the beginning of Charlotte aka Stone and other members of the SLT unexpectedly appearing outside my classroom or sometimes walking in, for no apparent reason. This had not happened before in all my time at Rokeby, but became a regular occurrence over the next few months.

I expected to be summoned to Charlotte's office that day to discuss the memo, or failing that later on in the week, but I never was. I consequently checked the register for that Media lesson – all students were present, and up to now, those students who apparently skipped class remains a mystery. I figured that she did not see it as important to clear my name, which made me feel even more undervalued and insignificant.

***

On another occasion, I was covering an Art class and had to use another classroom, because the Art rooms were being used for exams. The staff had been informed in the staff briefing that morning. I was two minutes late because I had to quickly organize my previous classroom.

Charlotte aka Stone was waiting outside the classroom. She said, "Did you not know about the room change?"

I replied, "Yes I did, but I am here now", and again, students were around us. I was made to look incompetent in their presence. I knew she was doing this on purpose, turning up wherever I was and reprimanding me in front of the students. There was nothing I could do about it, but remain professional and do my job to the best of my ability and get to lessons promptly in the future.

I tried to focus on the positive roles I had within the school and the fulfilment I got from being involved in the Careers advice, BPAP and Saturday school.

Trips

I have NEVER been on a school-organised trip with the students, despite me always showing a lot of interest in going. All teachers, Teaching Assistants, Learning Mentors and Administration staff have opportunities to go with the students on trips. It's regarded as part of your job, and it helps to see the pupils in a different environment.

For the 24th of June 2009, I organised a trip to go to Stubbers, the adventure playground, with the pupils from the BPAP. Two pupils had won The Jack Petchey award, and had been given £400 towards the trip. I did everything right, filled in the right paperwork and did it within the right timeframe etc.

Seamus Fox and Debbie assisted me, and at the time I said Charlotte aka Stone would NEVER allow me to go. Seamus was convinced I would be allowed, because he felt that this trip was important for the boys as it was part of a prize/reward that they had earned that I was part of. The paperwork completed, I put everything in Grant's pigeonhole.

It was returned a few days later, with a single yellow post-it note. Written on it was:

Please consider for next year

I don't know who wrote that; I blinked, not sure I had read it right. I turned it over, to see whether something was written on the reverse side, nothing, nothing to say why I could not go or who the note was from. I was hoping that the SLT and most importantly Charlotte aka Stone would give me this opportunity to go with the students, and if not with me, why not allow another member of staff to go in my place or even give the option to go on another day? I had to cancel the trip, to the students' disappointment, which did not make me look very professional at all.

Later that month Sarah Lawson spoke to me, regarding attending a National Conference about the BPAP. Sarah and I thought, it was a good idea that I went, because she knew I was passionate about BPAP and would have a lot to contribute and learn as I directly worked with the students. I had a feeling I would not be allowed to go though, and expressed this to Sarah.

Sarah proceeded to email Grant aka Useless, and he told her no. She tried again at the staff meeting, and he told her that Charlotte had said it was not necessary for me to attend.

Sarah was quite surprised. I was not; I said, "I told you!" You could see from her expression she just did not understand why I was being treated this way.

Timetable change

I liked this time of the year, because Year 11s had started to take their exams and most were concentrating on revision, so the school was less rowdy. There is always a sense of calm as the staff wind up the academic year. Most of Year 11 teachers were invigilating exams, dreaming of the upcoming long summer break and the various school trips, with the anticipated end of term drinks at the local pub.

I tried to ignore the hostility I was feeling at the school. I just wanted to do my job and help the students any way I could. I felt stressed each time I entered the green gates of the school, because even though I was doing my job well, I could feel a storm brewing in the atmosphere and felt uneasy. I could not wait until the end of term, taking one day at a time.

I approached my pigeonhole with hesitation every day, not knowing if a brown envelope would be there and what its contents would contain.

On Tuesday the 23rd of June, a memo was placed in my pigeonhole requesting the company of Cherelle and I to attend Grant aka Useless's office at 3pm that day.

"What could it be about?" Cherelle asked me.

"I have no idea, but hopefully it's something to do with the lack of proper cover from some of the departments," I replied.

We had been filling in diaries of the amount of cover given for each lesson by the teachers and when we had to provide and use our own resources over the last few months. I was hoping that he had a strategy in place, so there would always be work for the students to do, without relying on us.

We both had lunch duty so we could not dwell on the upcoming meeting, but I was uneasy for the rest of the afternoon.

What happened to passing someone in the corridor, stopping and having a conversation? Instead of emailing back and fro and writing notes here and there. Yes, it's a big school and everyone is busy, but it's about using that time more efficiently when you can. I had spoken to him when I was covering a PE lesson that morning and he didn't utter a word to me about no meeting.

Promptly, at 3pm, Cherelle and I knocked on his office door. We were summoned in and told to sit down.

Grant handed us each a sheet of A4 paper; on it was a timetable. We were told that Shelley and Ms Robinson had arranged this new timetable for us and it was to be EFFECTIVE IMMEDIATELY!

I looked at it and tried to focus on the details, but it looked so intense and I instantly did not see how it would work. Cherelle and I looked up at each other and back down to the new timetable. Just at a

SATURDAY JUNE 13TH, 2020

glance I saw that we were expected to do gate duty EVERY morning and after school!

More importantly, after school every day, we were allocated one-to-one reading and on Mondays I was to attend Year 7 meetings.

I couldn't believe it! I said to Grant in a voice that was a pitch higher than it should have been, but under the circumstances, appropriate for the situation: "What about the Careers work I do with the Year 11s and the BPAP?? I am NOT a puppet. Why was I not involved in creating this timetable?"

He just shrugged his shoulders, and looked at me. Cherelle, on the other hand, had not said a word, she was just looking at Grant and me and back down to the timetable, breathing heavily.

"And why must it be implemented now, right at the end of term? "I said in frustration, trying to get some response from him.

Grant finally said, "Ms Robinson wants a high profile at the school gates."

There were so many questions I wanted to ask, I didn't know where to start!

I could see that there were absolutely no free periods for the whole of the day and no allocated time in the mornings to look at the covers of the day, much less collect my cover slip. I put this to Grant, hoping at least he had thought it through. "So when do I do my resources and pick up my cover?"

No reply, because he simply could not answer. I said if he could arrange a meeting with Ms Robinson so we could discuss this, and slid the timetable across the table back to him.

We stood up and left his office; my head was spinning. What just happened??

Cherelle was clearly upset and so was I. It was the manner in which it was done and the fact that communication with our line manager seemed to be non-existent. Did he not understand where we were coming from and know why we were so upset?

My issues with the new timetable were:

Gate duty

At present Cherelle and I were doing this duty, once a week formally, but doing gate duty every morning is just too much! The school day is very precise. Apart from the students at breakfast club, most students come to school from 8.15 to 8.30 and go to their registration groups, where they stay until first period at 8.45am. Cherelle and I pick up our cover slips at 8.20am and between this time and 8.30am we both zoom to the various departments and classrooms to see what cover work is available. Sometimes this is the first the Heads of Department know that one of their staff is absent, so they try to provide something, or simply say they will put the cover work in the classroom before the lesson.

At 8.30am, if we are assigned to gate duty, we would join Brad, the police officer who was there every morning and a few of the SLT. Also, Debbie was there most mornings to make follow-up calls to parents and mark latecomers.

If I was not on duty, I would use that time to gather resources for the day – if no cover was available. I would also look for specific Year 10 and 11 students to remind them of their Career interviews with Connexions. Sometimes I would go to assemblies for the various year groups or give feedback to teachers about their classes I had covered. That time was valuable and to be used wisely as the school day is extremely busy.

At precisely 8.43am, we would then leave to get to the classroom, before the bell went at 8.45am, and classes would begin.

Previously we were given a timetable to see when you were allocated gate duty and who with. This new timetable seemed as if we were doing the morning duty on our own, which made me extremely worried about my safety. I had no problem interacting with the students, but being on the gates on your own with no back-up seemed ludicrous, especially as we were in the age of students carrying knives, hence the necessity of the school's resident police officer.

Grant aka Useless had said that Ms Robinson wanted more of a visible presence, or high profile at the gates. So, why not have Senior Management and Brad, the police officer there from 8.15am until 8.45am, like before, it just did not make any sense!

To have just Cover Supervisor on gate duty has no effect, because we have no real authority! The students knew we were not Senior Management, so when we asked them to, "Go home and change your trainers", or "Remove your jacket and give it to me, because it's not black", or "Get off the phone", they would simply look at us and unsurprisingly, kiss their teeth!

But if a Brad or a member of the Senior Leadership Team were in the vicinity, then there would be a different response. The students would reluctantly remove their jacket or come off the phone, muttering under their breaths as they made their way into the school, casting you a dirty look in the process. That, I could live with.

Briefings

My other issue with doing gate duty every day is, when do we attend staff briefings? This is supposed to be compulsory. Briefing was every Monday and Thursday promptly at 8.20am to 8.30am in the staffroom and in my opinion was quite important. The room was always packed like sardines; you were lucky to get a seat. Latecomers were frowned upon and tended to hover by the door, looking flushed.

Normally Ms Robinson would lead the meeting, and after saying her important announcements she would call on members of the Senior Leadership Team to make their announcements. Ms Robinson and the Senior Leadership Team had had a meeting before the briefing so she had a rough idea of who was going to speak and what they would say, and then after that she would throw the meeting open to anyone else who had something to say. You would put your hand up to be selected by her. It sounds quite chaotic but it worked, and everyone tried to be brief.

Many things are bought to light in those ten minutes. It could be that a fire practice was to take place first period, or that a parent of a student had just died. So to be sensitive to that student's needs. Maybe a specific student had a medical issue, so we were made aware of certain symptoms he might have. Or the IT department informing us that the computers were going to be shut down for repairs during Period 1.

Sometimes, it's at that time you hear a member of staff is leaving, or are introduced to a new member of staff, or that a baby had been born to a staff member, I could go on; it's a time that 99 per cent of the members of staff members are present. From Les the Caretaker to the Teachers. Administration staff to the Technicians. Teacher Assistants and even Mary the Librarian attended, just to name a few. It was a quick opportunity to touch base with everyone, before we all went our separate ways for the day.

During that time, Brad and a member of the leadership team would be doing gate duty and if you were rotated for Monday and Thursday, you would join them after briefing.

So what was to happen now? I was no longer allowed to attend staff briefings as I had now been allocated gate duty from 8.15am to 8.45am every day. I could not believe I had been excluded from staff briefings! Simply like that, discarded with a flick of the hand! Didn't Ms Robinson see that it was crucial for the cover supervisors to be present at briefing, especially as we were in the front line in classrooms with the students?

Periods 1-5

On this new timetable, all five periods of each day I was allocated a class that I had to be in if I did not have a cover lesson to do. Fair enough, a majority of the classes were in the Maths department which was my area of expertise and the rest in the Science department. My issue with this was there were no fewer than eight different Teachers on this timetable that I would have to liaise with and the lessons were spread from Year 7 to Year 10. I could not get my head around this! What was I supposed to do in those lessons? Was I supposed to teach or assist? And how was I supposed to know the contents of the lessons to be taught in class from each department? No time was given on the timetable when I was supposed to meet with those teachers, and how was I to know what each and every one of them required of me in each lesson, as all teachers have different ways of doing things.

What if I arrived at the lesson late because I was sorting out the previous lesson or had to leave the lesson early – how would that affect the students? Again, when do I check what has been left for the cover lessons I have to do? When do I prepare my resources? When do I write incident reports on situations that have happened in class? When do I call parents on the occasions that I have to? When do I give completed work to teachers and get some feedback?

After school gate duty

Again, five sessions are too much every week! Sometimes you need to keep students in, after the bell has gone at 2.45pm so the students can complete work that has been set or if they were late for the lesson. Sometimes, when behaviour was unacceptable a detention was one of the sanctions the school used. This was one of my tools and very effective during period 5, as the students wanted to be the first out of the gate.

I also used this time to arrange meetings with other members of staff or with parents and outside agencies like Connexions. I also completed any paperwork that had to be done.

After school activities

Having two cover supervisors doing literacy club in my opinion is a waste of resources. Especially, as we would have to identify the students and arrange for them to attend. How and when were we supposed to do this? Cherelle at the time had no commitments after school yet as she was just integrating into the school, she used to help me with the BPAP sometimes. She said she wouldn't mind doing the literacy classes as she wanted to be an English Teacher or a Learning Mentor, but she wasn't happy that she had to do it every day.

I, on the other hand, was furious! When I first started at Rokeby, I was encouraged to take up after school activities to integrate, which I did.

Mick Eyres had given me more and more responsibility with Year 10s and 11s, and when he left I was told to continue this work by Grant. Organising the Year 11s' career advice had established me within the school and helped me get to know the students. I have literally just redesigned the Connexions room in the Pastoral Building, which I use on Tuesday and Wednesday to assist the students in writing their CVs and filling out application forms.

I was currently getting the Year 11s to complete a survey so the school could track their progress during the summer holidays, whether they were planning on going to college, work or do an apprenticeship. I don't know who was going to work with all those students and take over all the activities I did with them – who had the time?

And worst of all to drop the BPAP is absolutely devastating! After how far Debbie and I had come with the boys, and how much work we

SATURDAY JUNE 13TH, 2020

and the boys had put in, it was just unbearable! This whole timetable change was a bloody nightmare!

The first person I spoke to was Sarah Lawson because of my concern about the BPAP being dropped. Thank God she was still in school.

I sat down in front of her desk with a heavy burden on my shoulders. I expressed to her that in our BPAP sessions we were trying to teach and show the boys respect. This was not a good way to demonstrate it by shutting the group down and at such short notice. She was shocked, because it was the first time it had been bought to her attention. Sarah knew how passionate we were about the students within the BPAP group.

Sarah spoke to Ms Robinson.

The next day she gave me feedback because she knew I was quite upset about the whole situation and eager to hear what Ms Robinson had to say. I would have loved to have arranged an appointment with Ms Robinson to discuss this, but it was just not appropriate and, moreover, Grant aka Useless was doing that, so hopefully I would get a chance to speak to her soon. Sarah simply said that Ms Robinson did not say to cancel the BPAP. Only that it needed to start after I had finished literacy club or the one-to-one sessions, so start the BPAP at 4.15pm.

I said to Sarah, "What do the boys do between 2.45 and 4.15pm? As going home and coming back would be senseless and they could not stay on the school premises unsupervised."

Sarah had no answer. She suggested I should look for another member of staff to cover that period. This option would have been difficult, because most staff have commitments after school already and I could not think of any available person.

You could see that Sarah was beginning to show signs of discomfort, at what she was observing with the dynamics between Ms Robinson and me. She chose, as many of the staff did, to ignore the situation, as it didn't directly affect her. Could I blame her? I myself, after all, didn't know why there was all this resistance to me and what I had done to deserve it.

I contacted Unison because I was concerned about the new timetable and the fact that I had been excluded from the staff briefings. I spoke to Steven Terry, the regional officer of Unison.

I said, "Ever since the email incident, it's been one thing or another constantly with SLT, I am feeling victimized, I don't know what to do anymore! I just want to communicate with them in a civilized manner and let them tell me what I am doing wrong!"

He asked what had been happening, I gave him a summary and finished with all the problems with the new timetable. All he said was, "If your hours are not changed then it's in the Head teacher's discretion in how ever way she sees fit how your time is spent."

I replied, "I know she has the right to change my timetable, but surely me being consulted doesn't change that, it just means that we can iron out any problems, and we can discuss the direction of the careers and BPAP work I do, also any problems she has with me personally."

I was trying to be optimistic. I asked him to be present whenever the meeting was going to take place with Ms Robinson, because I needed his moral support.

On the 24th of June, the new timetable was implemented. The timetable that had not yet been agreed was now plastered on the notice board for all to see and it had been emailed to the various staff concerned.

I started having teachers come up to me to say, "Why have you been put in my class? You could do the class without me??" (Laugh laugh!)

"What a waste of resources!!" they would mumble as they walked away. I just didn't know what to say in reply.

SATURDAY JUNE 13TH, 2020

1st day

Cherelle felt obligated to do the new timetable and started it immediately on the 24th of June. She said she didn't want to cause any trouble, as she had a child to feed and did not want to lose her job, which is totally understandable. I, on the other hand, was going to wait until I had seen Ms Robinson aka Stone before I started the new timetable. I did not want to fail even before I had started and give her an opportunity to sack me. I would respect her decision once I had the chance to put my point across. Hopefully, Grant would have told her my reasonable concerns.

So, Cherelle went off to do her morning gate duty alone and I went off to sort out my cover for the day. I did not find out until later that there was a fight at approximately 8.20am, Cherelle had tried to stop it, and been hit with a school bag. Apparently, the fight was so serious that one of the students involved was excluded. Cherelle was alone and did not know what else to do. Debbie had joined her later and commented on the fact that she had been visibly shaken.

Later on in the day when she had had time to reflect on the morning's events she wrote an incident report, which all of the staff would normally do when a fight takes place, especially as one of the students got excluded. She passed it on to Grant aka Useless, hoping he was not going to blame her for allowing the fight to escalate. She was clearly upset as she was telling me about it later.

I could not believe it! This was exactly what I was talking about! I take my hat off to her for doing the gate duty alone with no backup whatsoever. I felt extremely bad for her, because I should have been there, but so should the School's Police Officer and members of the Senior Leadership Team. Hopefully, Grant aka Useless would see my point now about being alone at the gates and talk to Ms Robinson aka Stone and the soulless Shelley about the necessity of having someone of authority at the gates, so this kind of incident does not occur again.

Even before this incident, with PC Brad and the SLT at the gates, there had still been serious fights. The mind boggles to think, why Ms Robinson aka Stone would think that violent incidents would decrease with Cover Supervisors at the gates. I do not know! It's like being sent to war without the proper equipment with only the Cover Supervisors being on the front line, with no weapons to protect ourselves. We were just pawn pieces on a chessboard, easy to get rid of and of little value.

I had never seen Ms Robinson aka Stone at the gates by herself, so why would she risk anyone else doing it? Yes, I could have been there, but I would have wanted some form of backup. I had been injured the first week I had started working at Rokeby in the *'dining hall'*. A fight had broken out with no SLT member present. I had tried to separate the boys, but got kneed in the knee, which was really painful. I could not walk properly for days; I knew then the importance of having the support of the SLT in keeping members of the support staff safe.

2nd day

The next day, on the 25th of June, Cherelle was at the school front gates at 8.15am ALONE again. I attended the staff briefing – Ms Robinson aka Stone had always stated in the past that all staff members must attend. After the briefing I collected Cherelle's cover and Debbie and I quickly made our way to the school front gates. I was hoping to see at least PC Brad there, especially after yesterday, but no one was there apart from her alone, poor girl! She stayed there till 8.40am and made her way to her first lesson, while Debbie covered the last five minutes at the gates.

I don't know how they expected her to get from the front gates to reception, climb the stairs, most probably two at a time, dash into the staffroom, avoiding colliding with other staff members. Then rumble through the mess on the table for her cover and then figure out that her first period is in the West building, gather her thoughts, thinking

SATURDAY JUNE 13TH, 2020

which way is the fastest route?

East – through the library and then English block; or west – backtrack? Pass the Maths rooms and go through the SEN department –risking dirty looks from the territorial staff; or worst option south – along the corridor, pass assembly and through humanities department and down the stairs, colliding with students going the opposite direction.

"Miss, Miss you are going the wrong way!" echoing from the students in the background and finally dashing across the playground. Against the odds, arriving at your destination on time, trying to regain your breath and composure, rummaging in your pocket for the key to the room so you can quickly look at the cover work before the students arrive.

Just as you are about to open the door, a friendly face says, "Oh, weren't you at the staff briefing, classes have been moved to the English block on the third floor!"

***

Since yesterday Cherelle had been trying to identify what she was supposed to do about the literacy classes that were listed on the new timetable. She had gone to the English department, but no one knew what she was talking about. They said, "All the students who have been identified as needing extra help, have all been allocated to either the SEN department or Karolina who deals with students with English as their second language."

So she went looking for Karolina, and caught her as she was just leaving her classroom. She was known for her abruptness. "You don't know their targets or levels, so how exactly are you going to help??" Karolina said quite irritably to her. It was obvious when Cherelle was telling me about it, that no one knew about this literacy thing it seemed apart from Grant aka Useless, Shelley and Ms Robinson aka

Stone; everybody else was in the dark.

***

That afternoon was to be the last BPAP as far as I was aware. I did not know how to approach the subject with the boys, as just the previous week we had been making plans to apply for more funding. Debbie could not do it alone because she had other commitments until 3.30pm; I was devastated. I looked around and saw Jesse and Kevin proudly in charge of the snacks – having everyone queuing in an orderly fashion. Mwanza arguing or I should say discussing with Hassan, and Bolade playing table tennis with Dolton without fighting. Chris entertaining the crowd with his jokes and impressions, and Callum and Nigel playing a game of Connect Four discussing relationships. I was so happy that they were respecting themselves and each other, and really appreciating having a safe place to hang out and socialise with their friends, as well as learning new skills after school. It would be a shame if it all ended now. They had grown so much, mentally and emotionally since being in the BPAP.

I decided not to say anything because I knew the first thing the boys would say is, "She's racist, Miss! I knew it, I knew it!" referring to Ms Robinson aka Stone, and it would take me forever to calm them down and convince them otherwise. I thought, hold on until you speak to Ms Robinson aka Stone yourself, hopefully it would be good news. Debbie agreed.

3rd day

On Friday the 26th of June, Cherelle was on the school gates promptly at 8.15am. Surprise, surprise she was ALONE again! – what happened to the high presence at the gates??

SATURDAY JUNE 13TH, 2020

Especially with what had happened two days ago. A fight broke out soon after between two students, Cherelle felt obligated to do something and in the process of separating the students, got hit on the side of her face with a school bag, laden with books.

Cherelle stayed there until I came to give her her cover slip for the day's lessons at 8.45am. As I passed it to her, I could see that one side of her face was slightly swollen. She briefly told me what had happened as we rushed to Period 1. There was no time for me to comment as we were both going in opposite directions, but I was lost for words and my heart was heavy. What a way to start the day for her!

***

Later on in the morning, at 10.45am, I was on break duty, which was at the front gates. It was a lovely day with a slight breeze in the air. There were three students milling around me, eating their mid-morning snacks. One of the boys was chatting to me about a programme that had been aired the night before, he had made a rather funny comment about it, and the four of us laughed. As I was about to reply, I saw Ms Robinson aka Stone marching towards me with purpose.

She looked quite angry and her cheeks were flushed. I presumed she was rushing out of school for an appointment and was running late. Instead, she stopped right in front of me, turned to the three students and told them to leave.

As they turned to go, she immediately turned to me and said, "Where were you during Period 2, you were supposed to be in Room 3?" The look on her face was of pure disgust, as if she had just trodden on something revolting and could not, for the life of it, shake it off.

I was taken aback by her approach and tone of voice, but I ignored it and replied, "If you are referring to the new timetable, I was waiting on an appointment with you, if possible?"

I thought she would be happy to see me doing my gate duty, but instead she hastily replied, "I don't know about that, but you need to follow my instructions, until you have an appointment with me."

I wanted to be professional and have this conversation in her office, instead of out here, but I had no choice, but answer, "I am not too happy with the new timetable, Charlotte; I would rather have an appointment with you first to discuss my concerns."

She then pointed at me; the tip of her finger was hovering in front of my face. "Are you saying you are not going to follow my instructions?"

"No, I am not saying that, I just need to discuss it with you further," I said quietly.

I could not believe she had her finger in my face, this had gone too far, someone hold me back please! The Vaseline would have come out to grease my hands in preparation for war. My earrings would have been unhooked and removed and my hair tied back. She surely would have found her backside on the floor, like we did back in the day – I had had enough, a finger in my face! Can you imagine?

Instead, I just looked down at the concrete floor, like a defeated, wounded animal. I tried to focus on the sound of children chasing each other and laughter coming from the playground and tried to feel like them – carefree, hopeful and enjoying the moment. For me I couldn't have felt more opposite, I had been stepped on and crushed into dust.

"Well, if you are not going to follow my instructions, then I will have to take the matter further." Her finger was still pointed at me, her voice was raised now and some of the students were looking in our direction. I wanted to end this conversation by letting a hole appear and swallow me up. I did not understand what she meant about taking matters further and by her aggressive tone and body language, I did not want to know.

I finally said slowly, "I can't stop you from doing what you need to do. You are the Head Teacher, but I would still like to discuss it first."

This was like my final plea. It was like I was begging for my life, because I knew she had the power to make my life unbearable at the school, which she had already achieved. It was a lose-lose situation. If I tried to defend myself, I would have been described as being 'aggressive' and my situation, guaranteed, would have worsened.

As she turned and walked away, I was feeling like a balloon that had been pricked and was deflating slowly. What just happened here?? What did I do that was so severe for her to be so aggressive to me in front of the kids? Plus, I am sure there are better ways to get your point across without intimidating me and making me feel so small.

Surely, Grant aka Useless had explained to her the difficulty I was having with this proposed new timetable and having it effective immediately! Did he not tell her about all the trouble that Cherelle had been having at the front gates in the last few days?

The bell went, signalling the end of break. I walked away from the front gate in a daze, through reception to Ms Robinson's secretary room and spoke to Denise to find an available time. She quickly scanned Ms Robinson's diary and arranged an appointment for me at 4.15pm later on that day.

Sunday June 14th 2020

Over in the States, protesters were angry about the death of Rayshard Brooks and showed it by turning out during the evening at the Wendy's restaurant where the incident had happened – they burned the building down! The footage was broadcast over the media all over the world. You could feel the frustration of the people as the flames took hold of the building with fury.

Meeting with Ms Robinson aka Stone
I kept myself busy once school finished, but kept looking at the clock, willing for the time to move faster. Most of the staff had left already, it was a Friday and there was a sense of eager anticipation for the weekend. I, on the other hand felt quite apprehensive, as I looked down at my questions that I had prepared for her on the sheet of A4 paper.

I had called Unison earlier to speak to Steve Terry (the regional officer), he was not in the office, and Keith (the Unison secretary) said he could not send anyone down to the school at such short notice. I was nervous, I really did not want to attend this meeting on my own. Debbie, my rock, had already gone home due to a family emergency.

Finally, I made my way down the stairs, along the corridor and knocked on Denise's door. She looked up with a plastered smile on her face. "Go into her office, she's expecting you." I muttered, "Thank you" and proceeded in the direction of the anticipated meeting.

I tapped on her door, and I heard, "Come in!" Walking into her office I tried to look confident, with my list of questions in my hand. Ms Robinson was sitting behind her desk, staring intently at a few sheets of papers.

I hesitated once I got through the door, but she signalled with her hand for me to sit down without looking up. Her eyes focused on the papers on her desk, my heart was pounding! Were those my marching orders to leave the school on her desk? I had not even had the chance to voice my concerns.

Suddenly my month was dry, I swallowed and sat down in front of the desk. I immediately felt like a student who had been called to the Head teacher's office to be reprimanded. I broke the silence by saying quite politely (because I did not want her to talk to me the way she had earlier):

My first question: "Just out of interest, Charlotte, why make this sudden change just before the term is coming to an end?"

This was a simple question. If she could delay the changes till next term, I could organise the BPAP, careers advice and meet with all the teachers I was supposed to work with. Until then, I would have to keep explaining and showing how I would find it impossible to do the Cover work effectively, plus gate duty, lunch duty and whatever else she wanted me to do. Hopefully, she would understand my point of view.

Instead, she said, "Staff were in the staffroom with nothing to do", which completely threw me – what a random thing to say, does she mean I have nothing to do?

I felt quite offended. I replied, "I don't know about them, but I always have something to do, maybe not even enough time sometimes." I continued, "If I am at any point in the staffroom it's because I don't have a classroom or office space, so I have to complete any paperwork or use the computers in the staffroom."

There was a brief silence and then she looked up and said, "It's in your contract to do 36 hours, have you read it?" She was flipping through my contract; it was a few pages, but she kept on doing it as if she was looking for a £50 note. I must say it was grating on my nerves, as there was hardly anything to read.

This was not what I came here for. We were supposed to be discussing this new timetable that she had devised, not my contract; and even if it was a discussion point, I was doing much more than 36 hours.

I looked away from her hands and tried to establish eye contact. I really wanted her to understand where I was coming from and tried to refocus my concerns and my questions back to the new timetable.

So I said, "But when do I do resources?"

She replied, shaking her head, "You should have enough resources by now. If not…"

Phew! I thought, so Grant aka Useless had talked to her about my concerns.

I was going to say, "If not… what?", but I bit my tongue.

Where does she think the resources come from? She must surely know that work I gave to a Year 8 class is different to what I would give to a Year 10 class. I work very hard to ensure that if no cover work is set by the Teacher, I provide age-appropriate work and that takes time.

I thought I would come back to that, maybe I needed to tell the teachers to let Ms Robinson know specifically that I do provide my own resources when no work is available and have done so for two years plus. Surely, she was aware of this because I have covered her own maths class and I had to provide extra work for them.

I decided to change tack and said, "So when do I pick up my cover, as I am supposed to be on the gates from 8.15am to 8.45am, and the cover is ready at approximately 8.20am?"

She replied, "I don't know, sometime before the bell goes."

I was trying to stay focused on what I came here for, but beginning to find it extremely hard, as she was talking to me in such a patronising manner.

I quickly added, "When do I pick up cover work?"

I did not get an answer as she referred back to the contract, that she had put back on her desk.

I then said, "Have you ever been in a classroom…"

She interrupted me, "Of course, I have been in several classrooms!"

"I was about to say, have you ever been in a classroom with no cover, as a supply teacher?" I was desperately trying to get her to understand where I was coming from, as a Cover Supervisor. If I had to cover all these classes; it just would not be possible to do my job properly.

I did not get an answer, and by then, I was feeling hot and frustrated. It was clear she did not understand where I was coming from and frankly by her bored and agitated look, she didn't give a damn.

I said, "What about all the things I do around the school?"

And she simply replied, "What DO you do?"

I could not believe what I was hearing! Did she just ask me that? I could not bring myself to answer. I thought to myself, this must be a wind up, surely? After all, it was under her authority that I was involved in BPAP, Career Advice, invigilation of exams, plus all my other different duties around the school, and of course Saturday school.

Then she said something random again: "The move to the Humanities department did not work out, so now you are part of the Science and Maths department."

The move, what move? Is she taking the mick? I replied, "That's because I only did photocopying for the teachers and since I have been here at this school, I have had no other form of career progression."

It had to be said, but she just ignored that last comment.

She went back to talking about my job description and hours; I could not get my point across. I looked down at my sheet of questions … I had gone off track, I wanted to ask about staff briefings, BPAP, but I was confused, my head was spinning! I tried to ask further questions, but when I tried to talk, Ms Robinson aka Stone would interrupt me.

I was getting quite distressed and told her that I was feeling bullied and victimized, to which she apologised, but instantly continued in the same manner.

She simply was not listening or hearing what I was saying. Why couldn't she see that I was an asset to the school? I was so thirsty to learn, and to self-improve, why couldn't she mould me and give me an opportunity to grow? What was so wrong with me that I could not be given a chance? Had I not proved myself enough? Was I that bad an employee, that she banned me from staff briefings and took everything away from me in that school that brought me joy?

Just like someone had seen the potential in her and given her a chance to climb up the ladder and flourish to have the confidence to be where she is now, why couldn't she give me a chance? What had I done to deserve this treatment? To be spoken to in such a derogative manner, like a shadow and not an actual living being with blood in my veins. I felt any dignity that I had left, was gone.

I could not believe what I was hearing. I looked at my notes and all the words started to blur and looked like an ink mess on the paper. This was my career, my life and she just kept dismissing what I was saying.

My chest started to become tight, and I was having problems breathing. In my mind, I thought I was having a heart attack, not that I know what it felt like, but what else could it be?

My breathing was getting worse, and I could not continue to talk. I remember watching her mouth move, but I could hear no sound, like the sensation you feel when your ears pop on a plane.

SUNDAY JUNE 14TH 2020

I remember Charlotte getting up and trying to touch me, as the look on her face had turned from being nonchalant to slightly concerned. I said to her in-between breaths, "Please, do not come near me, this is ALL your fault!" I remember stretching my hand to keep her at arm's length, just in case she had thoughts of coming any nearer.

Because this had never happened to me before, I think I began to panic, and this made it much worse. Parts of my body went limb, my notes dropped to the floor and scattered, I could hear myself say, "I can't breathe, I can't breathe!" Not sure whether I was going to pass out. I slowly fell to the floor, breathing hoarsely, clutching my chest. I was screaming in my mind, "What the hell is happening to me????" It was all happening in slow motion and there was nothing I could do to stop whatever was happening. It seemed as if I had lost control of my body.

I don't know how much time had passed. It must have just been minutes, but felt much longer. I just remember opening my eyes, I was lying on the floor in the recovery position and Leslie and Gurgit were talking to me, but all I could see was their mouths moving. I recall being given a brown bag and told to use it to regulate my breathing by Leslie.

In that first five minutes of coming around, I felt so exhausted and confused. I had the urge to vomit, but most of all I was scared. Had I had a heart attack? Or a stroke? My remaining hair was soaked through with sweat, my top was clammy on my skin and my shoes were halfway off my feet. Even though I couldn't move yet, my eyes darted around frantically looking for Ms Robinson as this was her office. I just wanted to get out of that room.

An ambulance was called during this time. As soon as I could feel my hands, I quickly touched my arms and thighs to make sure I could feel them; thank God I am not paralysed! Leslie was kneeling at my side, holding my hand and her presence made me feel safe. It took some time for my breathing to come to an acceptable level, and my pulse. I felt as if I had just run a marathon.

Hubby was called on my request. He arrived in ten minutes by taxi: out of breath, just after the ambulance people; he rushed into the office wanting to see me. The expression on his face was relief when he eventually saw me. The ambulance people told him not to worry, that I was going to be ok. "It seems like your wife has had a panic attack and passed out."

The lovely ambulance lady asked me, if I wanted to go to hospital. I was extremely worried as I had never had anything like this happen to me before, and didn't want to go through that again. I was not going to spend any time in hospital if I had anything to do with it – what would people think? Plus, I had too much work at school to do.

We reached a compromise, to have a check-up in the ambulance to make sure everything was working properly, meaning, my heart rate, blood pressure and pulse had to be back to normal before I was allowed to leave.

On coming out of the ambulance after approximately 20 minutes, I was so embarrassed! I could not believe I had collapsed in the head teacher's office. I was so thankful that all the students had gone home and a majority of the staff. Hubby and I sat outside on the bench underneath the mature tree in the cool evening breeze, by the science block, as I took stock of my situation. I knew I looked a mess, but there was nothing I could do about it right now, just breathe!

Mrs Oladitan, a well-respected Jamaican Humanities teacher, who was on the verge of retirement, was walking towards the car park. I had socialised with her outside of work and really had time for her, plus she always had sufficient cover work when she was absent.

She looked at me like an owner who had to put down their well-loved dog, because it was sick and way past repairing. "My dear, look at you, is this worth it?" She must have known what had happened as she could see the ambulance.

"You need to look after yourself; no job is worth risking your health for!"

She rubbed my back in a tender way. "Go home, and rest yourself, child", and with that she straightened up, smoothed out her blouse and strolled off towards her car.

She was right of course, but I did not know what to do, I was still in shock that I had had a panic attack, I was so weak, I just wanted to go home… to a safe space.

I heard later that apparently Ms Robinson aka Stone was seen sneaking out of the school, not wanting to give an explanation to Hubby about why his wife collapsed in her office. He was furious that she was not there, because no one could tell him really what had happened and I did not want to talk about it in detail. Just thinking about the incident made me very upset with my heartbeat increasing rapidly.

Doctor again!

Going back to the doctor to find out more about this panic attack was awful. I explained to him what I could about what had happened to me, but it took me a while, as I had to keep stopping and catching my breath. As I came to the end of my explanation, my face was dripping and my top was soaked; I had been crying and not really felt the tears.

Bless him, he sat and listened patiently and slid the small box of tissues in my direction. Not sure whether inside he was thinking, *'Get yourself together, woman, your 10 mins is up!'*, but on the outside, he looked concerned about me and my health.

"Judging by what you have told me; I am going to put you on anti-depressants," the doctor said

"What are you saying, Doc? I have no time to be depressed, I have bills to pay and duties to undertake at work, my students need me…"

"I am afraid for you, you need to have a rest, I will give you a sick note and we will review how you are in the next few weeks. I will give you some medication to assist with the sleeping and anxiety."

"Also, Doc, more of my hair is falling out." I took my wig off so he could see what was left.

"It looks like you might have Alopecia?" the doctor said, looking at my scalp.

"What is that?" I was clueless…

***

After that I had no choice but to face reality. I felt like shit and physically looked like shit to put it mildly. Hubby dropped me off at school so I could leave my sick note in Grant's pigeonhole. We intentionally went early in the morning, roughly 6.30am, so as not to interfere with the school day. Also, I was not up to seeing anybody in the state I was in.

I didn't really care about anything else at the time and felt guilty not being at school. I could talk about nothing else for hours on end. It's hard to explain, but the school was like a family because you spend so much time together. You get to know the staff really quickly, you socialise with them, you support them, you celebrate their highs and lows, so not seeing anyone and being able to talk about it was so difficult. I could not keep burdening Debbie about it, because she still had to work there and have some sort of relationship with the people who were hurting me.

My skin had broken out in a rash and because I was stressed I picked on them, which made it worse. My hair continued to fall out. My scalp was just patches everywhere; I did not feel womanly at all. I had to do something about my health, but what?

During the first week, I had several missed calls from Grant aka Useless between 6 and 7.30pm –outside of work hours. Initially, I thought it was to check on my wellbeing until I received the text below from Grant aka Useless at roughly 7pm one evening.

> Hi Shola needed to let you know a few things, 1) when you are signed off you should not come on to the premises this could result in disciplinary action. 2) Now you reached trigger 2 for attendance I will need to arrange a meeting with occupational health for you, have tried to call but no joy.
>
> Please call if you wish to discuss further. Grant

I did not see what the problem was, as I recalled I had been on the school premises to drop off my sick note. How could I foresee those rules, I have not been on sick leave before?

I honestly did not believe I had done anything wrong. Many members of staff that were on sick leave came into the school during the working day. Julie Kennelly, the admin lady, when she had an operation, came into school during lunch several times during her sick leave. Jean Cooper, the lady who worked in the SEN department, was always in, even though she was signed off sick. Willie Deigan, the drama teacher, that injured his back, was always popping in. This was just to name a few and none of them had been reprimanded, all white members of staff, of course!

Discuss what? He had not wanted to discuss anything with me the last few months. He was quite aware of the distress I was under, but did nothing to make my situation better. Even though he was in a position to make a difference. He was just as much to blame, and now he is referring me to Occupational Health (OH) and basically saying if I was seen on the school premises again I would be reprimanded! Can you imagine?

This made me feel that I had done something wrong and had been excluded from the school premises. The whole situation was upsetting and distressing for me. Since the text did not require an answer, I thought it best just not to go on to the school premises again and to attend the OH appointment – whenever it was arranged for – instead of engaging with Grant aka Useless and becoming more upset.

In the following days, I received a recorded delivery letter from Grant. The text he sent me was pasted into the letter, as if after he pressed the send button on his phone and thought, "Oh… That's not very professional; better pop it in a letter, in case she does not have enough brain cells to interpret the text message."

Also, the letter was to inform me that a meeting with the Occupational Health Worker was going to be arranged. I did not understand why I had to see one, but I was so drained, and like I said before I didn't have the strength to have 'a discussion' with Grant aka Useless.

Nowhere in the text or letter mentions, "Oh… so sorry to hear about your illness, Shola", or "how are you? Hope you are getting better, Shola", or "let us know what we can do to help, Shola, in your recovery". None of that, just so cold. You would think I had just started working there! During those three weeks, no one from school inquired about my health, not my line manager, Grant aka Useless or Ms Robinson aka Stone. Call me old fashioned, but if someone collapsed in MY office, or more importantly a member of MY staff, the least I would do is make sure they were ok, even if my secretary did it on my behalf. It just shows that they really didn't give a toss about me because I was that person that was insignificant.

Hair again!

During those three weeks of sick leave, I tried to make sense of what had happened. Every time I thought about it, I would get wound up and start having problems with my breathing. I was so scared that what had happened in Ms Robinson's office was going to happen again. I was not sleeping well, despite the medication and was waking up in cold sweats. Hubby encouraged me to go and update Steve Terry from Unison, about everything that had happened and the proposed OH appointment.

My hair at this stage looked like a scarecrow. I found it hard to look in the mirror at myself, I didn't realise my body was going through such trauma. I said to myself:

"There are people literally starving in Africa and you are worried about your hair!"

But Hubby said, "Look you have no hair in the middle of your head and the sides, you need to try to even it out."

"I know, it's awful, I don't know what to do!"

Then Hubby said: "I know you don't want to hear this, but I think it's best just to shave everything off and start again…"

I glared at him for even thinking about it, but I had no choice, I really did look ridiculous.

"Ok, but take it easy…"

He went to get the clippers and I tried to prepare myself. I was shaking and tears had started to build up and drip down my face, this was so emotional for me.

I blew my nose and kept touching my head and feeling my remaining scarce hair.

As soon as the clippers touched my head, I flinched. "I can feel it! It's too low!" I shrieked and moved my head.

"It's on grade 0, so it WILL touch your scalp, but it's not painful, just relax, you will be fine."

I knew he was right, he was always right. I had to close my eyes as he proceeded to gently shave all my remaining hair off… my identity. I could feel the clumps fall on my shoulders and then onto the floor, lifeless, useless to me now!

"Oh my God, I am bald!" As I felt frantically for any remaining hair, it's done, I really have no hair!

My scalp felt strange, smooth like a baby's bottom. Looking in the mirror I could see the shape of my head and it definitely didn't look attractive to me. I was alarmed, asking myself 'Who is this person?'.

"You still look sweet," Hubby said.

I don't bloody feel it!

My hair never grew back the same again, but I was not to know that at the time. If I had faced reality, I believed my hair was damaged and toxic right from the roots after all the trauma it had been through indirectly. I knew I would have to rock this look for a while. On that day I felt so low and lost, without my hair – who was I anymore??

Union

I had tried so many times to get hold of Steve Terry from Unison, the secretary Keith would either say "oh, you just missed him!" or "He is in a meeting, not sure what time he will be finished?". It was a nightmare! So I demanded that a meeting be set up, somewhere in Steve's diary, so I could ask him what to do. This was an emergency; my job was on the line. With reluctance Keith looked at Steve's schedule and arranged a meeting the following week.

Finally, I was so ready for this meeting. Steve Terry, the regional manager, listened to me explain what had happened and I finished with the fact that I had to go to the Occupational Health Worker. I was in tears by the time I had finished. You could see from his drained expression, behind his glasses, that he had heard so many of those type of tales, nothing surprised him anymore. Whereas with me, this was happening to me right here and now, it was a first, I was feeling every word I spoke, and I wanted a solution from him.

He sat there in his chair looking at me, shuffling the papers again and again, then he finally said:

"You have to go to the Occupational Worker, the school has the right to send you there."

But, how will I cope till then? I am due back at school soon, I thought, please do something, anything, don't let me go back to the same nightmare!

"What about the camera footage? When she was pointing her finger at me? Are you going to ask for it from the school?" I had remembered this, surely if anyone sees that footage from that day, by the front gates, they would surely come to the conclusion that this was not the way to talk to your members of staff.

"Let's get the report done first, we can take it from there." Shuffling the papers again was him telling me the meeting was over.

Help please!

I wanted to speak to someone else about this situation, but who? I wanted to do something about this injustice, but what? If I was to make a formal complaint I would have absolutely no idea where to start. I had managed to get my hands on a hard copy of the Disciplinary and Grievance procedures. Having to go to the Occupational Health when there was nothing wrong with my work performance made me so upset. I felt as if I was being bullied and on top of that denied the opportunity for career progression, it just was not fair; there must be something I can do?

Fare well Saturday school

The kids at Saturday school were asking to see me. I was really sick, I could not even get out of bed, but Debbie said they had got me flowers and wanted to give them directly to me. It took all of my willpower to get out of bed, I couldn't even have a shower. I just wore my slippers and morning grown, I got there and I stood outside by the gates. It was so awkward, the kids had to come right up to the gate.

"Why can't Ms Sandy come in?" I heard Lazarus say to Debbie with a puzzled, but concerned, look on his face.

Tears fell down my face. I was trying to keep it together, I knew I missed them, but had not realised how much. I felt so weak and, as an adult, we are not supposed to appear weak to children. I couldn't control myself, it was genuine concern from them, all of their tiny faces with pure joy in seeing me, speaking through the gates like a prisoner to a visitor. I bent down so I could be at their level. I could only come out with:

"Thank you so much, this means so much to me."

I was barraged with questions from the children.

"Why can't you be here with us?"

"Are you sick?"

"Why are you crying? Don't you like the flowers?" Sheridan said, a cute, dark-skinned intelligent girl.

"No…no, don't mind me, I love the flowers! They are absolutely gorgeous!"

My heart was torn that day. I remember it clearly as if it was yesterday. I loved the gorgeous flowers, but hated the pain and despair I felt once I received them. Somehow, I had a strange feeling deep in my heart that I would again never be with those lovely kids in that setting.

Writing my grievance

After talking to a few members of staff about my situation, I was told to contact Tom Alexander from Human Resources. I was so relieved to be speaking to someone outside of the school gates, who could intervene on my behalf and take an independent view. Hopefully, he would be my advocate and resolve the situation once he knew all of my concerns.

SUNDAY JUNE 14TH 2020

I called and gave Tom a detailed account of what had been going on, he listened, am sure he could hear that I sounded quite distressed. I also told him about the video footage of Ms Robinson pointing her finger at me.

"Can you access it before it's deleted, I have already told my union about it?"

He said he would look into it, he took my email address, so he could email me an electronic form of the updated grievance procedure so I could submit my complaint in the right format.

Reading through the grievance policy, I had already tried to resolve the situation informally. Firstly, by speaking to my several line managers and then by asking the union to be involved. Finally, bringing my concerns to the Head teacher, but to no avail. So now I would have to go to the next stage, which was to submit a formal complaint against Ms Robinson aka Stone.

After going back and forth, I really did not want to do this, but I wanted and needed to be treated fairly in my workplace. If someone from her peer group could just talk and reason with her, surely she would come around and see my point of view?

Looking at the blank piece of paper, I just did not know where to start. Julie was a trusted friend of mine and former employer that I had worked with as a Personal Assistant back while I was at university. She was always so kind and supportive of my studies and was so proud of me when I finally qualified as a Mechanical Engineer. Julie was more like family and had a calming effect on me to focus on the task at hand.

Julie had so much experience in dealing with conflict management using her diplomatic way of thinking to diffuse any situation. She said reassuringly, "Just write what has been happening to you since you started working there and whom were the people causing you distress." Julie said she would assist me to word it in the right way.

When I sat down to actually start to write, I found it very difficult to put into words what I felt was happening to me at the school. I could not believe I was in this situation. The hurt and pain I felt was unbearable, I wanted to fix whatever was broken, so I could be left to just do my job! Once I started writing, it all flowed out and I felt clearer about what my concerns were; with the help of Julie, she made it look presentable.

I hoped and imagined an external party would come in, once I initiated the process, talk to Ms Robinson, members of the SLT and me separately. Look at whatever evidence was available, speak to relevant witnesses concerned and make a decision on how to move forward. I typed up my handwritten grievance that I had gone over with Julie, prayed and submitted it to Tom Alexander from Human Resources.

Union meeting -17th of July 2009

I met with Steve Terry, the regional officer from Unison to let him know. He was not happy about me taking the matter further. I remember thinking to myself, "Isn't he supposed to be on my side? Why is he being so frosty? Could he not understand my frustration about not being treated fairly?"

But I reassured myself. With his position as regional manager, surely he would be able to influence the conversation with the school and perhaps try to encourage them that I needed to complete the training course this September among other things. Maybe, he just needs time to compose himself. I know that I can be quite full on; either way, I was uneasy with his lack of enthusiasm. Especially, as I had had the successful experience of working with Jay (also from Unison) when dealing with the signing in/out incident earlier in the year.

Going back!

On my return on Monday 20th of July after three weeks off on sick leave I was quite apprehensive. I stepped out of the staffroom after the morning briefing, Ms Robinson and Tracy Ward – one of her soldiers – were talking about me and I distinctly heard my name mentioned.

I had my back turned as I was heading down the stairs. I can't believe they are talking about me, knowing I would be able to hear them. With a sigh, I said to myself, 'God give me strength for the next three days!' It felt like being a child back at school, where the bullies would snigger and murmur as you walked by, all laughing at precisely the same moment, hoping for you to trip over your shoelaces and fall flat on your face.

I just kept on walking towards the school gates for morning gate duty, hoping my shoelaces were tied and I wouldn't trip up. Ms Robinson aka Stone came up to the gate and directly addressed me. I thought she was going to ask me why I was not at the gate for 8.15am or why did I attend staff briefing, as she had just seen me leave the staffroom. Either way, I was feeling apprehensive as she spoke to me.

It occurred to me that she might say, "Oh Shola, good to see you back, I am glad you are feeling better. I have thought about the concerns you raised at the meeting and am willing to listen to your issues with the new timetable and hopefully find some solutions."

Instead, she said, "How are you?"

Is this a trick question? – I thought, does she really want to know? Or is she setting me up for something sinister.

"Ok, thanks," I replied, considering the circumstances I wanted to add. I was waiting anxiously for whatever she was going to say. I tried to summon something similar to a smile, but could not manage one.

"Do you know what group you are in?" she asked me. I knew she was talking about what was happening for today – the staff were being split into groups for staff training, the list was already up on the notice board and I knew where I needed to be.

"Yes, Group 2, in the English Department," I replied.

"You are in Group 2," she said.

I thought to myself why bother to ask me, if you are not going to listen to my reply. She did not say another word to me. I was glad other members of staff were present. I felt safer with other people around; we all stayed at the gates till the bell went.

On Tuesday the 21st, we had sports day; we were not on school premises. I was most probably more excited than the students, as I had never been on a school trip before and seeing that EVERY staff member and student was going, Ms Robinson had no choice but to let me go.

It was held at a sports centre, just off the A13 motorway. All the staff were wearing casual wear and spirits were high, even the moody kids were smiling. The stands were packed with student spectators who were cheering on their classmates and staff encouraging their students to do their best.

Grant aka Useless and Ms Robinson aka Stone were clearly talking about me. News had obviously spread that I had submitted a grievance and both of them had been implicated. I could feel the negative smog of energy directed towards me. I wanted to stay on the down low and just do my job. So, most of the day, I spent supervising the long jump and triple jump, way over on the other side of the sports field where all that negative energy couldn't reach me.

On Wednesday 22nd, the students just had two lessons. Strangely, I had to cover the two lessons, most probably because I was the more experienced between Cherelle and myself.

Both lessons I actually had NO classroom for the students, as both allocated rooms were being used, so I had to find some space for the students with great stress to me. Imagine walking around with 25-plus kids looking for an empty classroom, absolutely hilarious! I would have just stayed in the playground, if not for the football match that was going on at the time. I managed to survive both lessons only to be told that a meeting was going to take place at 11am.

During the meeting Cherelle and myself were informed that Grant aka "Useless" was no longer our line manager due to other commitments and Grant aka "Pastor" was to take his place.

I thought, Useless knew of his commitments before he introduced the changes to our timetables, so not only do I have a new timetable, I also have to now explain to the new line manager my issues with it.

Not only that – hold on to your seats, people – another timetable was given to me! This time with different lessons (I don't know whether any teachers were consulted about this one either!).

Also, gate duty had changed from 8.15-8.40am (giving us 5mins for what exactly, before first lesson, and who made that sudden decision?).

Changing my white line manager to a black one, makes me feel as if I can't be managed by a white person, and this simply is not true! I just needed things to be fair, this was just all simply madness! I had never been so happy to end a school year!

Anyway, this was my formal complaint that I submitted, which most probably explains the frosty attitude from Stone, Useless and the rest of the SLT.

> My name is Shola Adewale Sandy. I have been employed by London Borough of Newham Education Department since January 3rd, 2007 till current time. My workplace is at Rokeby School, and my post is that of a Cover Supervisor. I was recruited according to the job advertisement at Scale 5; however, my initial contract stated Scale 4.
>
> I believe I have been experiencing harassment, bullying and victimisation at work. I believe that additionally, this has involved racism and sexism.

I wish to formally take out a grievance against Head Teacher Charlotte Robinson on the grounds of bullying. This has taken the form of:

1.Persistent criticism and humiliation both in public and in private.

2.Rescheduling work so that it becomes impossible to achieve.

3.Delegating me repeatedly to do unskilled work at the expense of my contracted tasks and of my required breaks.

As a result of raising queries regarding the above, I feel that I have been punished.

I wish to formally take out a grievance against Finance and Systems Manager, Shelley Eckton on the grounds of harassment. This has taken the form of:

1.Undeserved embarrassment and humiliation by the publicly sent email in which I am described as, 'probably on drugs'.

2.The sudden requirement and insistence on me to 'sign in' last year, when not all members of staff have to do so.

I also wish to formally extend this grievance to include bullying in the form of:

1.Rescheduling work so that it becomes impossible to achieve.

I wish to formally to take out a grievance against Assistant Head Grant Leppard who acts as my current Line Manager. This has taken the form of professed ignorance of my contracted work, lack of supervision, failure to monitor my work in the agreed manner, and failure to support me in attempting to resolve operational difficulties with the timetabling of my duties.

I further wish to formally complain of experiencing harassment by him through the repeated telephone calls and text messaging to my mobile phone, 'out of hours' i.e. after 6pm whilst I have been off on sick leave.

I have brought all of my concerns to the Head Teacher and have received no positive response.

I have been denied opportunity to undertake training and therefore seek promotion. I have remained on the same level of pay at which I started my contract. Any attempts to seek further training have been refused without good reason. The alterations to my timetable have resulted in me needing to work additional hours to those I am contracted, in order to achieve deadlines and complete my work. Additionally, I have worked outside of my contracted hours in the past in order to undertake additional tasks. This has been unpaid and unrecognised.

I believe that I have experienced treatment different from my colleagues, specifically that of a white man who commenced employment in the same post, at the same time as myself. He has been supported to train and gain promotion to a Learning Mentor, with back payment. I believe this to be less favourable treatment.

Overall, I have experienced constant undermining and harassment as I attempt to undertake my work. This has now become the climate of my workplace.

Although I have attempted in the past to resolve these difficulties through informal meetings and letters, this has been unsuccessful. I have emerged feeling humiliated and disempowered. My anxiety and stress levels have risen during these repeated encounters. I am now off of work through ill health and on medication. The situation has now deteriorated to such an extent that I am left with no other recourse than to formalise my grievances.

When you appoint an Investigational Officer, I will supply evidence and names of Witnesses.

I look forward to hearing from you when an investigation date is sent.

It may have sounded severe, but I wanted whosoever was going to look into it, to see that this was a very serious matter, difficult and uncomfortable conversations had to be had to resolve it.

Monday June 15th, 2020

All everyone was talking about was that image at the weekend, *'a black man carrying a white man, out of danger'*, it was in all the main newspapers and spattered on the news channels all over the world. The hero's name was Mr Patrick Hutchinson; he was giving interviews to the media and rightly so.

He said in one of the interviews that if one of the three observing officers that witnessed George Floyd's death, did what he did, then maybe George's life could have been saved. Thankfully, Patrick Hutchinson was there at the protest with his mates for a reason they would never have imagined. He works as a personal trainer by trade and is a grandfather. It was his intent to protect the young black boys and girls attending the rally from the far-right protesters. He never would have believed he would have been in the position to save one of them. I think that's why the image was so shocking, as he could have easily turned the other way. I know if it was me what I would have done...

It was so good to hear his thoughts on Channel 4 news later that evening:

"I just want equality for all of us, at the moment the scales are unfairly balanced and I just want things to be fair, for my children and my grandchildren." He answered to one of the questions directed to him.

I am still not aware whether the white gentleman came forward to privately or publicly say thank you to Mr Hutchinson for lifting him out of danger, only time will tell whether he will do the right thing.

***

Today, all non-essential shops will be opened in the UK, provided those shops can enforce social distancing and hygiene guidelines. Hopefully, it will be nothing like the IKEA queues on the 1st of June where people dashed there to queue for over three hours! But, it seemed everyone was just happy to be out of the house today and doing something different, despite the inconvenience.

***

Today the government has announced it will have commissioned a new report on Racial Inequality, due to be released sometime in December 2020.

"Hey, Boris, I am here to contribute… I'll be waiting for the details!"

We have had so many inquires over the years. The McGregor-Smith review into *'Race in the workplace'*, *'The Lammy Review'* by David Lammy MP, *'Windrush Lessons Learned Review'* by Wendy Williams, just to name a few. But, what we need from all of these reports are the recommendations to be implemented and monitored.

Summer holidays

As well as having to attend the Occupational Health meeting, I received another letter from the school dated 22nd of July 2009, to say that I was invited to attend a grievance meeting on the 9th of September 2009. I quickly read through the letter and was horrified to see that Ms Robinson aka Stone would be present – what hope did I have now??

I don't understand why she had to attend herself. Was she trying to intimidate me? After all, I was complaining about her and her

MONDAY JUNE 15TH, 2020

treatment of me. She was like an arsonist, investigating the case of a fire after setting the fire herself in the first place. I just can't believe she will be there and leading proceedings!

Occupational Health meeting – 4th August 2009

As part of this damn process, I was told I needed to see an Occupational Health worker. I did not know what to expect and to be honest I was a bit nervous. I just hoped I would get some help with dealing with what I was going through. It was early August and it was a lovely sunny day, people were dressed for the weather with a lot of undesirable feet and skin exposed. I wore black trousers, flares, and a dark brown blouse with my shiny black, recently polished Doc Martens (by Hubby, of course!), had to be comfortable as I was not sure how much walking I would have to do.

As we came out of Royal Albert station on the Docklands Light Railway aka DLR, I asked for directions and we steadily made our way towards our destination, Newham Dockside. I was amazed at this big overwhelming building in front of us. It was mainly constructed of glass, seemingly in the middle of nowhere, which you just could not miss!

The sound of aircrafts could be heard and seen cruising in and taking off from the runway at City Airport. Everyone seemed to be heading out or coming from this visually overpowering place. It was the first time I had come here; I understand that it was affiliated with Newham Town Hall which was based in East Ham.

I presume in order for Newham Council to save money, they had decided to move most of the services from around Newham to this new building. God knows how much was spent, but it didn't look cheap. I personally didn't agree, as I liked the convenience of services being kept locally. Years ago, if you required the council services, you could just pop into an office by Stratford Station (which I think is now a school) or into Stratford's Old town hall. It was accessible to all, not just chucked in the middle of nowhere, where it became a destination spot and nothing else.

Anyway, I was told in the letter to report to reception in the West Wing (sounded like something out of *'Dynasty'* or *'Dallas'*. We walked into a huge open foyer area, which was used for reception. From there, we were directed to take the lift and came out at the appropriate floor, where we were then told to wait in a small office to be called for my appointment.

I really did not want to be here; it was the summer holidays, I should be carefree, hanging out with friends and family; instead I am here having to talk about distressing things. My stress levels were palpable and felt I was no longer able to cope mentally with those people I happen to work for. I did not know what was going to happen in September, it was all I could think of. I was praying for a solution, preferably a miracle, hopefully from this person that I could not stop thinking of since I received the confirmation letter.

After waiting approximately ten minutes, we were shown into a spacious room with floor to ceiling glass windows overlooking City Airport. The view was breath-taking and I took a minute to take it all in.

Dr Occupational Health worker was a pleasant enough lady; she proceeded to explain why I was there:

"I have been asked by your employer to ask you questions about your job."

I shifted in my seat.

"What do you think you need in order for you to be able to do your job?" The lady looked nice enough and I felt encouraged to open up.

"What the hell, what do I have to lose!" I thought to myself. "How can I do my job properly with Charlotte making my life hell??"

"What do you do on a daily basis?" she asked to start me off.

I started from the beginning and poured out everything that had happened. She would stop and ask me questions, I guess she had to tick boxes. I could clearly see she was getting more and more uncomfortable while listening to my story and shifting in her chair. While I began to relax more, I broke down my day and she could clearly understand that I had a lot on my plate and did not feel supported.

I wanted her to say what she was going to do in order to solve my problems. I tried to speak slowly and concisely, but I was clearly upset by what I was going through. Tears flowed down my face, but I kept focused, as I wanted her to understand the facts and the order of events.

"What difficulties are you having?" she said sympathetically as she passed me tissue upon tissue, bless her, when I blew my nose loudly and continuously, like an elephant. I am sure my sneeze caused her soul to jump out of her conservative body as well as the foundation of this glass building! "What was the frequency needed to smash glass?" I thought mindlessly

"What can be done in your opinion to improve your work situation, as it does not sound good?" She was shaking her head from side to side.

Are you kidding me! Of course, I know that! I wanted her to say she was going to call Stone up and curse her out and tell her to do the right thing; instead, I shrugged my shoulders when she repeated herself.

I breathed in, blew my nose again and finally said, "I just feel if someone independent with some influence looked at my situation, they would see the treatment I have received has been unfair. They would be able to help me... I think?"

At the end she said she was going to write a report, which would be ready within a week or so and send it to my line manager. In my mind, I was praying the report came before I started back at school in September, hopefully it would recommend putting me on the TA course immediately and propose a way to move forward with my timetable.

She also recommended counselling sessions for me, she brought out a booklet with contact details of counsellors offering their services in Newham and the neighbouring boroughs.

"I suggest you contact one of them straight away," she said convincingly.

Why do I need to go for counselling? Is that stating that it was me with the problem? I just did not understand why I had to come for this meeting, getting myself all upset in the process and now I am being sent to someone else? When will this problem ever be resolved??

"Thank you." I hesitantly took the counsellor information she passed to me.

I had never been one to go for counselling. If someone had told me a year ago I "would be considering going for counselling" I would have laughed so loudly, and told them "Absolutely impossible"! "But now I might actually, possibly consider it!

Coming from my type of background, I didn't know anyone who had counselling from my community. We were just too busy hustling, trying to live, with no time to sit down, discuss or dwell on our issues as bills were piling up all around one by one, needing to be paid.

Obsession

During this time, I felt that I had no control over anything to do with work, all I could think about was:

"What am I gonna do? What am I gonna do?" The only thing that I could control in my life right now was the fact that I would have to have basmati rice every SINGLE day. I had a special small pot I would boil it in and I would just eat that alone. If I ran out of basmati rice in the house, it was like the world had come to an end!

The process of making it was important too. I had to use fine sea salt to get the required taste. It had to be boiled for a specific time, with me hovering over it during the cooking period.

And it wasn't just any basmati rice, it had to be from Tesco (other brands are available), there was a specific taste and more importantly it came in a purple bag and purple is my favourite colour, bizarre right?

While I sat and devoured my rice, all was well with the world and me. I would try to make it last so that feeling stayed, but as soon as I got to the bottom of the pot, the dreaded feelings would come back and take me over again.

That would be my dinner and sometimes breakfast, and on the worst days it would be both breakfast and dinner, crazy right! But it didn't seem like that at the time.

Handling folder in – late-August 2009

I felt so much anticipation and belief when I went to drop my folder for Tom Alexander at Newham Dockside reception. "All will be well!" I kept repeating to myself, as I walked towards the building.

The folder had become quite detailed as I did not want to accuse someone of something without showing examples and proof. Everything that is written in this book thus far are all real and all on public record. From names of staff, letters to emails, general correspondence, witnesses, other victims and of course my contract. So, whoever ended up looking at it would have a clear picture of my complaints. Of course, as a stationery fanatic, the folder had to have proper sections with coloured, numbered dividers with a contents and appendix page so you would know where to find what you were looking for. It felt great to finally hand it over. All that hard work, compiling it and now it was finally over and out of my hands. I was hoping and praying that whoever's lap it landed on would jump up and take action straight away.

Time to chat

School was starting this week, I thought I need something to get me through the school gates; Hubby said call the counsellor, maybe she can suggest something to help you…

I remember thinking: "What a waste of time, black people don't do counselling, we don't have time to be depressed!"

Hubby would often say to me, "One hand can't clap", meaning you can't expect to solve your problem alone, without talking about it." I didn't agree, because I hated telling people my business, I always thought I could solve my problems alone.

But Hubby had convinced me – "What do you have to lose? Go. If you don't feel comfortable, you can make your excuses and leave, plus it's free, so take advantage of the service!"

What can this person do that I haven't done already? A little voice in my head said, "Just give it a go, what do you have to lose?" So I looked at the various options and picked someone based in Ilford, which is just next door to Stratford. Thankfully, the lady had a slot available, so we arranged for me to pop down for a session.

On the day, I left plenty of time to get there as I did not want to be late. I turned into the road which was just off Ilford Lane and walked approximately to the middle, looking to see the door number I wanted. I pressed the bell and waited nervously.

A smiley white-haired lady opened the door. A relaxing familiar waft greeted me. I felt immediately at ease. She led me through her beautiful home to a room at the back. A strong smell of lavender was in the air and hit my nostrils as soon as I walked in the room. There were house plants strategically placed and right opposite were doors leading to a plant-filled garden. She told me to sit down and get comfortable. There was a glass of water on the table for me and a box of tissues.

After some pleasantries, she said:

MONDAY JUNE 15TH, 2020

> **C:** First of all, I would like to say that anything you say in this room is confidential; also, I want you to remember I personally cannot solve anything, but give you the tools to help you find a solution.

What does she mean? I thought, I hope this is not a waste of my time, surely she will be able to do something, when she hears all the things I have been going through.

> **C:** I would like you to be free while you are here, what would you like to talk about?

I didn't need to be asked twice. I launched into what had recently happened in Charlotte aka Stone's office, when I collapsed. Also, the fact that the recent Occupational health worker recommended the counselling sessions when she saw what a mess I was.

I looked at her to comment on what I had been saying for the last 10 or 15 minutes.

> **C:** I need you to breathe, Shola.

> **Me**: What do you mean?

> **C:** You are talking way too fast, slow down, like this…

She proceeded to show me, how to take air through my nostrils and out through my mouth and feel my chest when I was doing it. I felt light-headed, but slowly started to regulate my breath. I had never done that before and all of a sudden, I felt vulnerable and open, but ready to talk again.

> **C:** Can you continue now, what led to that moment…

Me: I was doing my job, which I love and that has been taken away from me.

C: And how does that make you feel?

As I went into how I felt as a person, lost, confused, missing my school family, students, staff, I was in tears.

Me: I am so embarrassed! I shouldn't be crying like this!

She directed me to take a tissue from the box, which I did to wipe my eyes and blow my nose.

C: You need this, let it go...

More water came out of my eyes, than I ever imagined was there. I felt it from the core of my stomach, I cried and cried. What was wrong with me? CONTROL YOURSELF, WOMAN!

C: I want you to know that it was not your fault.

Me: Pardon? I said, through the tears.

C: It was not your fault.

It was the first time, I had heard someone who was not linked to the school, did not know me, had nothing to benefit from the situation, when she said that, I thought, what, surely I must be to blame?

C: You did everything right, you are not to blame.

I looked at her through the tears, with a newfound light and thought, what if she is right? Maybe she is right!

I left her house a different person after just ONE session, somehow managing to find a slither of peace in that moment.

September 2009

I returned to work at the start of the school year. Hoping that the one counselling session would see me through this war zone I find myself in; instead, I struggled to manage. Everywhere I turned there was someone from management. I was being watched from every angle, just waiting for me to fail at something, anything, it was making me so uneasy, affecting my mental and emotional health in such a negative way. I felt such a weight on my shoulders, every step or move I made seemed to require so much more energy, of which I had little to spare.

The report from Occupational Health had indeed been received by all concerned, but none of the recommendations advised by her had been implemented by the school. So the ridiculous timetable stood and there was no talk about any career development either, or me being put on the TA course for this year.

I nearly forgot to mention that during this time I was offered an amount of money which equated to three months' wages, with the condition that I ceased working at the school immediately. Obviously at the time I was offended by the offer – I did not understand why they had chosen to go down this route. It didn't solve the problem and meant I would be looking for employment at the same level in a different school. So the past three years' experience would have been wasted in my opinion, plus I didn't think I could present myself in the best light to another school right now. My confidence had taken such a serious knock.

Steve Terry from Unison thought it was a good idea and seriously encouraged me to think about it and accept the offer. I did think about it for about two seconds, then I said as politely as I could to him "No, thank you!".

A few days later the offer had been increased to six months' wages with a good reference included. Steve by now was exasperated and didn't understand my refusal when I got back to him with a second polite "No". I tried to explain to him that "It's about the principle, Steve, believe me it's not that I don't need the money, but when it's all gone, I will still have to live with my decision that the way I was treated was acceptable and in my mind that simply does not sit well with me!".

All of this was taking a toll on me. I kept experiencing heart palpitations, scared to think it would lead to further panic attacks. I decided the best thing to do was to see my doctor. He advised me again about my stress levels and without hesitation put me on sick leave from the 7th of September. The school and union were obviously fully aware that I was on sick leave as I informed them both. I was hoping that with the grievance coming up that it would get postponed until I got better and returned to work; after all, I was the one who had requested the grievance in the first place.

In the meantime, they had my folder. I was sure investigations were already going on regarding my case and I was gearing myself up for someone independent to call or write to me wanting to ask me further questions about my allegations. Hopefully, I would get the opportunity to expand further. This would also give them a chance to view that infamous video with her finger in my face and ask her to explain herself!

ACAS

With all the drama going on, I was looking for an external party to support me as I was not getting the expected help I needed from Steve Terry from Unison. This organisation ACAS (Advisory, Conciliation and Arbitration Service) sounded so promising. I called them up as I wanted them to be involved and find a solution that worked for both sides. I got the impression that they wanted the other side to push for it more and that was not happening, so that avenue was a non-starter, unfortunately.

2nd time Counsellor – 15th September 2009

I desperately needed another session from the counsellor. I was getting quite nervous as I had heard nothing from HR or the school about the date the grievance had been postponed to. Also, why has no one been in touch regarding the contents of my folder – did no one want to ask me any further questions?

I was so relieved that the Counsellor could find a slot for me, it was great to be able to talk about me and my work issues for that short time I had with her. I knew she was being paid, but she looked so interested and focused on me. I could be free to talk, no matter how insignificant I thought my problems were, she always would raise it up and say my problems were important.

I told her about the folder I had handed over and how upset everyone seemed to be.

C: If I was you, I would try to look for people that can help you outside of the school system.

I only had six sessions with this breath of fresh air, only four left now, how will I cope without her? How can I get more sessions? I needed her, I can't think of going on without these ideas and words of encouragement from this wise lady!

I treated my sessions like gold bars. Unfortunately, I found out I was not entitled to anymore and I certainly could not afford any, so I tried to spread them out. It was like getting an energy shot each time I saw her. Needless to say, I am a convert now, in speaking to counsellors. I was able to let everything out without being judged. I was lucky enough to have had a really great one and she helped me to see outside of myself in a non-judgemental or patronising way.

Grievance decision

A few days later, I received a letter from Charlotte Robinson aka Stone dated the 17th of September with Tom Alexander from HR and Steve Terry from Unison copied in. The letter was attempting to address ALL the points I raised in my Grievance letter and folder.

Charlotte aka Stone said in the letter she would address ALL my points and then went about denying or having vague explanations to every point I raised. I was in so much shock. I could not believe what I was reading! Do you mean the 'they' and the 'them' was Charlotte aka Stone all along! How could they, as in HR, allow her to investigate herself? I simply do not know how she could come to those conclusions without any external investigation. The same answers I got from her at the last meeting is what I am reading in this blasted letter, so "What was the point in raising this bloody grievance?" I cried out in exasperation!

I am not sure what investigations took place from the first time I had contacted HR to the date I received this damn letter. Did the Grievance meeting take place as arranged, or was it postponed? In any event, nobody discussed any of the incidents with me or even bothered to contact me for a suitable alternative date. So many questions! I was so confused! What was I supposed to do now?

I felt as if I had been deprived of the opportunity to talk about my concerns and consequently, my attempts to amicably resolve this matter were even more frustrated by this latest move.

I was so distraught that I called an emergency meeting with Debbie and Esther. I needed some sisterly love and advice from people who understood the people I was having to deal with. We dissected Charlotte aka Stone's response letter with wine and some good carb snacks, trying to come up with ways to move forward. It was so unbelievable and so unfair, we had to laugh – what else could we do??

Saviour!

I didn't know what else to do, who do I turn to for advice? Was anyone going to understand the impossible situation I was in? I tried to contact local leaders within the borough. I thought if Charlotte aka Stone had one of her peers talk to her, maybe she would listen. I had heard through the community a gentleman called Jenkins that worked for a local organisation; apparently, he had been an advocate to many and had made a real difference to their lives. After several calls and attempts to meet, my chance came later in the month on Monday the 28th of September.

As Hubby and I waited for our turn to see him in reception, I was filled with renewed hope. Here was someone with a fantastic reputation for helping individuals within the borough. I had created a duplicate folder and gripped it tightly, going over its contents in my head.

As we walked into his office, which looked like a mini library, with books and bundles of papers on every available surface, normally I would be engrossed with my surroundings, but I kept on saying to myself "Stay focused, don't mess this up, Shola".

Jenkins came across as a pleasant man, rounded in all areas, especially his belly, but who am I to comment on that?!

Me: Thanks for taking the time to see me! I blurted out.

He invited us to sit down, I don't think my backside hit the chair before I started to spur out the details of my case. Obviously, I was upset and in tears already. I still could not talk about my situation without getting emotional thus tearful.

He just encouraged me to talk, nodding occasionally, listening to me intently.

When I got to the contents of the grievance letter, that I had received and the fact that Charlotte aka Stone had denied everything and practically investigated herself, I stopped to wipe my tears away with my sleeve, not dignified, but I was in the moment and the tears kept on flowing.

> **Jenkins:** That sounds terrible, I cannot believe you have had to go through this. Leave your folder with me, let me go through it.

> **Me**: "I would really appreciate that!" Hope at last! I was smiling, even though my eyes were sore and my head was banging inside. I felt he understood why I was so emotional. I handed him the folder that held the contents of my life for the last three years. I felt a wave of relief.

> **Jenkins:** I have an urgent meeting now; can I get back to you?

> **Me:** Of course, let me know what you need in the meantime...

I left there feeling a ray of sunlight, maybe, just maybe he will be able to help me…

Sick note

As soon as my doctor saw me again, he extended my sick leave. He looked really worried for me, I really appreciated his concern. By this time, I was on medication for depression, also he gave me some different sleeping pills to aid the amount of sleep I was getting, which was hardly getting any at all. I really did not want to get addicted to popping pills as a solution in the long term, but right now I had no other choice.

Saviour-decision meeting

That week or so went by so slowly. I couldn't wait for the meeting to hear his response. We arrived early on that day to make sure we used the time Jenkins had generously given to us purposely.

After sitting down and pleasantries, he coughed and I waited in anticipation, thinking we would make a good team. We can use this time to hatch out a plan, where do we start?

> **Jenkins:** As much as I understand what happened to you is unfair, listening to you and reading all the facts, you have a strong case; but I simply cannot help you... it would be a conflict of interest as I work for the borough too.
>
> **Me:** Oh, that's such a shame!

I didn't know what else to say. He was right, he could not compromise himself, but that still did not take away from the fact that I was extremely disappointed.

> **Jenkins:** The Black Members' Union may be able to help you, I know they have a lot of experience in these types of matters,

here are their details. Also, if I was you, I would appeal the grievance decision... I wish you good luck!

I felt so deflated when I came out of that meeting – Good Luck! I don't bloody need that! I was not angry at him, just frustrated to be back at square one.

He was my last chance. I needed an advocate, I needed someone to take action, someone to speak on my behalf, and now I felt more alone than ever.

I contacted the Black Members' Union in the borough for further advice. I was told there was a meeting coming up and would I like to attend.

"Of course!" I said, and I quickly wrote down where and when, but the meeting was not till next year. In the meantime, God knows what was to happen to me!

I even called up Race Equality in Newham for advice. I wanted support in the appeal process, if I went down that road. I was really surprised at their response, just by the name I thought they would be horrified and offer me lots of solutions and support. Instead, I was told even though they understood my predicament, they really could not be involved as it was a 'conflict of interest'.

I was really disappointed that they could not help.

Absences

Meanwhile, the school was going after me for my absences due to my sick leave. Grant aka Pastor summoned me to the school to inform me that disciplinary actions have been triggered. He repeatedly asked me why I was off and when would I return.

I just looked at him, I didn't know what to say, here was an intelligent man, in fact a man of God; he was pretending he was not aware of my situation, could he not see how sick I was?

As he frog-marched me off the premises quickly, if he was asked he would say *'walked me to the gate to stop me chatting to anyone'*. It felt so surreal, watching the children playing without a care in the world and members of staff going about their business, doing a double take when they saw me. None of them were aware of the trauma I was feeling inside. I remember being one of them, but now, I was beginning to feel like an outsider.

Occupational Health again! – 10th November 2009

It was actually scheduled to be on the 14th of Oct, but I had to rearrange it to the above date. I just could not deal with it. I was close to breaking point then. Why did I have to go for another Occupational Health meeting? It wasn't even the same person, so I had to explain everything all over again. Nothing for me had changed, in fact it had got worse. It felt like I was living in a parallel universe. No one was listening to me! I think I was in the process of having a nervous breakdown just trying to get my point across!

Union meeting 13th November 2009

I urgently wanted Steve Terry to let me know how to approach the appeal for the grievance and the relevant questions to ask. I took a set of questions to him to address all the points raised in my grievance and Charlotte aka Stone's reply. He made notes and told me the ones to rephrase and also when to refer to the folder. He was going to expand on my points at the right time in the grievance appeal meeting and talk in the relevant jargon.

Grievance appeal 25th November 2009

I had saved my last counselling session for today in the afternoon, so I could arrive at the meeting, calm and ready to put my point across.

The meeting was at the school. One of the things I had insisted on was not to have the meeting in the same room as I had had the panic attack. Thankfully, they had listened, and we were in one of the rooms opposite her office.

We were all around the table, it was big, but not big enough. I felt Charlotte's aka Stone glare and negative energy trying to penetrate my positive and optimistic aura. I purposely didn't sit directly in front of her, I shuffled my papers and practised my breathing technique, as the Chair started the meeting.

Tom Alexander from HR was sitting next to her, which threw me, as I had spoken to him in confidence back then, not realising he was in her corner and supporting her and not me. It all became clear now why the video of her pointing her finger at me aggressively had never seen the light of day.

I remember him, leaning into her with familiar ease, whispering advice. The set-up looked like I was the one who was being accused of something. You would never believe it was me who bought this case to everyone's attention.

It was the first time I had met one of the Governors, Ted Sparrowhawk. I expected him to be more proactive really and ask questions. He seemed to be ticking a box just by being present, and sat there looking bored.

I still wanted to be respectful – after all, she was the Head teacher of the school. I wanted to be reasonable. I wanted to find a way to move forward. I put some of my questions to Charlotte aka Stone, expecting Steve from Unison to follow on; he didn't, just silence. I thought, 'Why is he not saying anything?' I was left to continue but he had thrown me off. I tried to cover all the grounds, referring to the folder, but I could see I was just talking to a wall. I was asked one

MONDAY JUNE 15TH, 2020

question in total from everybody there, something about the weather? I came out of the meeting, simply bewildered by the lack of interest and engagement of such wrongdoings.

We went outside. Thankfully it was dark so Steve from Unison could not see the glare I was giving him. I looked at him in a totally new light – by him not saying anything, said a lot. I was extremely furious, what was his problem or agenda? He was the union for God's sake and a regional officer at that!

"How could you just sit there and not say anything to back me up?!" I asked him.

All I heard was mumbling from him as if he had swallowed a bottle of superglue, not allowing himself to have any eye contact with me. I was so disgusted with him; I could not say anything more…

I received a letter the very next day, postmarked, dropped through my letter box – imagine that? How is that possible? They must have connections in the post office was my only explanation!

I would have thought an investigation takes much longer than 24 hours. How many people did they talk to? Who did they talk to? Why did they arrive at certain conclusions? Who asked the questions? How was the investigation recorded? I did not expect it to be a 'Murder She Wrote' type of investigation or a 'Law and Order' as nobody had died (at least not yet). But maybe more time could have been given to gather the evidence and contemplate on arriving at a conclusion. Deliberating the facts and weighting it up to how they would have expected to be treated if they were in that situation. It felt like none of that had taken place and they were quite proud, it seems, to have turned the investigation around in such a short period of time.

I expected the governors to look at my rotas and timetables. Talk to students involved in any incidents I have mentioned and to speak to other members of staff. This takes time. If I was one of the governors, I would be embarrassed – after all, what was their role, if not this? I would have relished the chance of clearing my head teacher's name if I was one of them. They just remained quiet and clearly agreed and were happy with her conclusions.

So the conclusion in the letter, was that '*after careful consideration, the committee therefore found your appeal was not to be upheld*'.

When we look at when the Government commissions investigations, it takes forever for them to come back with their findings. I am not saying that their investigations were thorough, but at least it looks somewhat believable. Actually taking time to gather the evidence, not this third-rate rubbish!

Steve Terry from Unison did not seem to want to answer my calls. It was weeks before I got hold of him after the appeal that dreadful evening. I was upset – why was I paying the Union dues every month without fail, directly from my wages and now that I need them, they are nowhere to be found?! I think he just wanted me to go away and that was not going to happen!

I tried to get advice from other Unison workers, but it all came back to him as he was the regional officer. My hands were tied and now I had run out of options.

What was I supposed to do now?

Absences again – December 2009

I was summoned again by Grant aka Pastor for another meeting. My absences were mounting up, so the next stage had been triggered. By then I knew there was nothing more I could say or do. My grave plot had been selected and the grave diggers were at present digging the hole.

Believe me, even after everything I had been through, I still wanted it to work at Rokeby. I didn't think I would find anything else that could compare to the family I had created there. Was I being unreasonable to want to talk about it and find solutions to make it work? There was no mention of how I would be supported, and he didn't refer to the latest Occupational Health report or the recommendations, which, by the way, were the same as the first one.

Toynbee Centre

Steve Terry from Unison was not forthcoming on the next steps to take. I had asked him several times what to do after the grievance appeal hearing and whether I was entitled to legal representation if I decided to take it further. I had a strong suspicion that he was purposely avoiding me, what a surprise!

I was hitting brick roads at every corner! Someone who was feeling my pain said to me, "Why don't you try The Toynbee Centre? They offer free legal advice on such employment matters."

Get there early, so you have a chance of seeing someone and maybe be one of the chosen few, who gets someone to assist them with the paperwork and if necessary represent them in court. Once the numbers were reached, the doors were closed with a smiling but regrettable face and that was your chance of getting free legal assistance blown for another week.

That evening it was raining. Thankfully there was an overhead, so Hubby and I could queue without getting drenched. There was a bitterly cold breeze hitting my exposed face, making it difficult to focus for the hours that we were waiting and willing the centre to open.

Toynbee was a charity, fundamentally created for social reform in the community. It was based on Commercial Street near Aldgate East Station. They provided lots of services for the local people. This included free legal advice. It was always extremely busy, so when the quota of people were in, the doors were closed until the next session.

I remember queueing up with all the other desperate people. Everyone had a story to tell, everyone had had a miscarriage of justice.

Everyone was looking for free legal advice and a majority of them were well-deserving. We chatted and listened to their cases as we ourselves waited.

This was my third visit to the Centre. Each evening dealt with specific areas of need. The first time I got the wrong night, after waiting in the queue for hours. I think it was immigration issues. I was upset, but this is the price you have to pay. The next time, the quota was filled, so the doors were closed just before they got to me. I was devastated, but what else could I do?

Tonight was employment. I had checked and I got there extra early. I hoped I would see someone who knew what they were doing. I held my chunky folder close to my chest, hoping this time I would get to see somebody who would be able to help me. Fingers crossed, I would be able to explain clearly my case and why I needed assistance urgently.

I was extremely lucky to be directed to Sabrina. She was a young lawyer, who looked like the type of person who was paying her dues to the underprivileged community. Sabrina led me to a corner table. I remember subconsciously appreciating some privacy as I knew I would be emotional going through my story. After listening to me, trying to summarise my situation, all the while she was going through my folder. I held my breath waiting for her thoughts, and with no hesitation she said:

"You have a strong case, Shola; let's start to fill the forms required to begin the tribunal process, as time is running out."

I breathed a sigh of relief with tears in my eyes. Finally, someone believes in my case, someone believes in me, enough to do something about it! I wanted to hug her! In fact, I think I did!

Sabrina patiently helped me fill out the paperwork. One thing we had to do was to complete an ET1 form, which summarizes my complaints. She explained to me that I was the 'Claimant' and the London borough of Newham were the 'Respondents'. Sabrina clarified that because Ms Robinson, Shelley and Grant work for Newham, I was indirectly taking on the borough. I worked for the borough too; it all didn't make sense, but it was the only way. Sabrina did not understand why Unison was not helping me and I could not explain either.

Sabrina kept on asking me "What was the last straw, that broke the camel's back?". I found it hard to pinpoint a specific moment, as so many things had happened. Was it the new timetable introduced or the fact I had not been put on the course again? Or the fact that they kept on sending me to Occupational Health, as if I was not competent to do my job? We went with the unproductive meeting that I had with Grant aka 'Pastor' recently when he basically said, things for me would remain the same.

She told me the process could take over a year and I should consider, how I would cope if I remained working in that environment knowing I was taking my employers to tribunal. Also, Sabrina let me know what the next steps would be once we submitted the ET1 form.

To be honest when I started this process, I just wanted to take Charlotte aka Stone to the employment tribunal. I did not realise until later, it would be the borough I was taking to court with the limitless resources that they had and with the financial ability to back themselves. Even though we both worked at the school and for the borough, I felt I was at a huge disadvantage already, but at least I had a legitimate person who believed in my case, finally!

Time to leave the building!

It was now end of term. Newham had switched on the local lights, but Leyton's Christmas lights always made me smile more, especially those intertwined in the trees by Draper's Park, which seemed to sparkle as you go past. It was chilly and crisp but there was a buzz in the air as people were rushing around preparing for the festive break.

Decisions, decisions! Do I just move on and leave or remain working at the school, while the tribunal took place, however long that might be? Charlotte aka Stone and her crew would make my life a living nightmare, I am sure of that!

I wrote my resignation letter, feeling like a long-time prison inmate being released and forced into general population. Scared to leave the prison to go out into the world and experience the unknown, but know if you stayed, your health, family, friends will suffer and you would lose the person that you once were. Especially when I felt so low within myself – and let's not forget to mention the financial impact that this decision will have on my life – but I simply had no choice. I could not continue to live like this. I had to hand in my resignation.

The reply

This is what I received back from Charlotte aka Stone in reply to my resignation letter:

> I accept your resignation and will pass a copy of your letter to HR for processing. They will send you written confirmation in due course. Please return your keys and the main gate fob to the school.

That was it, after three years of working my butt off at the school, three sentences, but what did I expect? She must be so happy to see the back of me, finally!

Tuesday June 16th 2020

The only good thing about lockdown is that over the last 100 days we haven't had any live professional football games – peace and tranquillity. Yippee!

I was so thankful to be able to watch and listen to my BBC shows without the constant updates or the takeover when the games are live streaming. For others, they were jubilant at the prospect of football starting again, even though no fans were going to be allowed into the stadium to watch the matches. There will be an option to play crowd noise over the live matches to create some sort of atmosphere on TV for the adoring fans at home.

In the midst of all this, today Marcus Rashford who plays for Manchester United received a telephone call from the Prime Minister to congratulate him for the work he had done in his campaign. Marcus had recently written a letter to MPs requesting that the free school meals for kids should continue during the summer break. He had a lot of support from the public and even though the government refused initially, they did a U-turn and decided to fund the summer scheme. In my opinion that was mainly due to that letter and how Rashford came across.

This will make a difference to so many children and their families. I have witnessed kids coming to school without any breakfast, so they rely on the meals that the school provides during the day. The school holidays are always a worry as you don't know how those kids are coping so them having this during the summer break is an absolute life-saver for those kids and their families.

Everyone was so impressed with Rashford, including me. He really did not have to get involved, but he understood and could relate because he used to be to one of those kids who suffered from food poverty and now he was in a position to do something about it.

***

Racism in football is still a problem. Before the pandemic, you would hear regular sport news items like: bananas being thrown at the players or the chanting racial abuse at black players during games which was just not necessary. After all it was just a game, wasn't it? Even though there have been initiatives along the way like 'Kick it out', I am not sure it has been effective in dealing with racism in football.

The highest paid footballer I think is a black player called Raheem Sterling. I remember hearing about Sterling who is on top form and plays for Arsenal. He has had a lot of negative press written about him in the national papers over the years. It got to the point where I think Sterling had had enough and came back at the media. Recalling articles where he compared a black player to a white player in relation to how they were both portrayed in the media. When both bought houses for their respective mothers, the black player was portrayed as 'splashing out' and his motives were questioned, whereas the white player got comments that portrayed him as a proud son to have.

When looking at it like that, you could see his point of view – Sterling was just asking for fair publicity for all players, regardless of colour.

When I watch football on the rare occasion, all I see are the majority of the players are black, but when I look at the managers, it's a different story. This is exactly the same scenario in education in 'inner London schools' from my experience – so many black staff

TUESDAY JUNE 16TH 2020

but that's not reflected in the Senior Leadership Team. I overheard a football fan say recently "We hardly have any black managers of clubs", even Sterling has said there are not enough black managers.

When I researched this there were only six non-white managers out of the 92 English professional leagues. I do not understand this, as there are plentiful famous, great black ex-players – why aren't they becoming managers? For example, Ashley Cole, Dwight York and Sol Campbell have fought hard to get their Coaching/Manager qualifications and struggled to get opportunities, but the positions offered seemed to be few and far between, if any at all. Even if they were offered the roles, would they be supported whilst in a Managerial role? Would they have the option to be a Manager with clubs higher in the Premier League?

Whilst it seems to me white players like John Terry, Frank Lampard and Steven Gerrard seemed to get fast-tracked and offered roles automatically with hardly any experience once they stop playing.

Also, when footballers retire, I think they are used as "Pundits" on sports channels, but seemingly after a year or so, you don't see them anymore. Anytime a black face is needed for an opinion the same faces are bought out time and time again – Rio Ferdinand, Ian Wright and John Barnes, love them, but where are the others?

I came across 'The Rooney Rule' which was introduced in 2019 in the UK. To be honest, the only thing I know about any Rooney is Wayne Rooney the football player and the whole hair transplant fiasco, but that's another story!

But that's not the Rooney that introduced this rule. It was a gentleman called Dan Rooney, who worked for the National Football league aka the NFL as chairman for the Diverse Committee. He spearheaded a policy that clubs in American football should interview at least one Black, Asian and Minority Ethnic or BAME candidate for each head coach or senior football operation vacancy; this was in 2003.

Anyway, this rule states you must interview at least one black, Asian or minority ethnic candidate when searching for a new first-team manager in the UK. It does not mean you have to HIRE them, and it does not apply to Premier League teams – why is that? Come on, people, we simply need more black managers in Premier League roles, sort it out!

As of May 2020, the NFL are expanding 'The Rooney rule' to give more enhanced opportunities and executive positions for males and females. More ideas are constantly being discussed to increase the diversity. Which is a great thing, as whatever happens in the USA seems to trickle down to the UK eventually!

The same fan said, "We do not have any black football club owners in the UK." I thought that was interesting – why is that?

I don't understand why a group of black players, ex-players, pundits can't come together and purchase a club, even if they don't have the funds. Nowadays people are crowd funding for all sorts of things. I would really support that, if it happened, even though the politics might not make it easy for them to make it happen.

In America, they do have black owners of American football and basketball teams, so are more likely to hire black coaches or managers, because they may have the same vision and some sort of invisible trust is there. Come on, people, now is the time to club together and invest in buying a club, so we can have a say at the table!

January 2010

New year, new you? I was lost, on medication, feeling depressed, not being able to sleep properly. It seemed I did not have a purpose anymore. I could not do the job I loved or be around my school family without them feeling uncomfortable. I contemplated taking my life – after all, what was there to live for anymore? But then I think of the people who have been supporting me through all this, how could I do that to them? But in reality I don't think I could do it. I could not give them the satisfaction of knowing that all they had done to make my life hell had finally worked. I couldn't give them that pleasure.

Also, bills were piling up. Brown and white envelopes coming through the letterbox daily and the phone was ringing constantly for outstanding amounts to be paid. What was I supposed to do for work?

I had applied for several jobs; I was desperate, I even applied to the local supermarkets but they said I was 'over qualified'. Can you imagine? I said if it's not bothering me, why is it bothering you?!

Meeting Steve Terry 22nd February 2010

Finally, I secured a meeting date, now he knew I had submitted a ET1. I desperately wanted to know whether I would be entitled to legal assistance from the union. He said not all cases can be supported, it depends on the resources available and whether your case had a reasonable chance of success at tribunal. He would speak to them and get back to me. I wasn't holding out any hope, judging from his demeanour.

Newham Unison Black Members group – April 2010

I went for one of their meetings and fortunately was able to speak to someone, one on one at the end. After giving him a brief summary, he said:

"To be honest with you, we are so bogged down…"

I knew then that it would be difficult to get any help from them. Judging by the meeting, they had way bigger issues to be dealing with like group disputes, than my miniature individual problem.

Teacher training – Canterbury July/August 2010

I had kept the shaven look as my hair was not growing properly and I had managed to ween myself off the medication. I was trying to sort my life out, the only thing I was confident about was my love of Maths and the hope that one day I would be teaching it in some way, shape or form.

I was broken and washed up, holding on to some driftwood in the ocean when Filomena Kettlewell "The Angel" came into my life. She held on to that driftwood and firmly brought me back to shore.

I was applying for teacher training with the assistance of my friends as they, for some strange reason, believed in me. I was not the conventional student. I was older and coming from lived experiences, not like the young, springy students coming straight out of university. I was not sure whether I would be accepted this time as I had been rejected some years before. With my distinction at Birkbeck, though, I was feeling slightly confident – yes, can you believe it, a distinction!

I went for the Post Graduate Certificate in Education or PGCE option, my chosen university was East London. The demand for the course was so high, I didn't stand a chance; I didn't get into my second choice either. I had not even thought Canterbury would have been an option as it was miles away in Kent. But they were running a programme in Essex, much closer to me, and were looking for a cohort of students. For some reason or another, our paths crossed and I got called in for a formal interview and to sit some tests.

This was a whole-day thing. I was so nervous, as all I could think about was being a Maths teacher and to be given a chance. When I got there, it was packed with other potential candidates. I remained focused and completed all the tests including an intense Maths test. Some candidates were dropped at this stage, soon. The remainder of us had formal interviews with three people on the panel including Filomena. Question after question, it was all a blur, all I know was I was absolutely exhausted after it all. My brain literary felt fried!

TUESDAY JUNE 16TH 2020

I had the phone by my side all evening waiting for that call, checking and re-checking. I put the phone on the highest volume (anyone who knows me knows I only like it on vibrate or the lowest volume possible). Eventually, the phone rang and I jumped out of my skin at the sound of the ring as I was not used to it.

Ring ring

Filomena: Evening, Shola, I just wanted to let you know with great pleasure you have been accepted on to the programme!

I was not sure whether I had heard her correctly.

Me; What! Really! Are you sure??

Filomena: Yes, Shola, we will send you more information by email about the start date.

Me: Thank you so much!

As I put down the phone, I still could not believe it, did that just happen? Oh my God, am I really in?

I was buzzing for the rest of the evening. I had finally been accepted. Yippee, I am actually gonna be a teacher!

***

Filomena was the course leader for both Maths and Science. She was a petite lady with a huge presence and personality. She was firm and stern, but also kind and compassionate, the kind of person I was in awe of. Filomena led some of our sessions, especially the heaps of administration and the several assignments. She let us know that she was there for us, but also to prepare ourselves for the hard work we had ahead of us.

Our main teacher was a lady called Sarah Imbush. She was the Head of Maths in a girls' grammar school in Southend. Wow! I thought! I loved her style and the way she conveyed information to us. She made us work hard because she had high standards and she wanted us to have those high standards for ourselves and for our future students.

I remember the first time I met my fellow classmates during the summer of 2010, I felt like an imposter, surrounded by so many intelligent people and then there was me…

Tim, he was from one of the Russell Group universities. He was talented and within two weeks of starting the course with us, he was snatched up by a private school. He didn't even have to complete the course because the school didn't require him to. It came with accommodation too; it didn't take him long to figure out the better option. Tim said his quick goodbyes and was out of there like a shot!

Emma was a grammar school kid, through and through. She looked and spoke the part, she was the teacher's pet and always had all the answers. Her specialised area was Maths A level. Emma also had 'to die for' stationery: glitter pens, smelly erasers, cute pencils and varied sizes coloured post-it notes in a desirable pencil case.

Cerys was a very creative and artistic person. She would have done well teaching Art, but chose Maths and struggled at the beginning as she had to improve her subject knowledge. Cerys persevered and improved due to her work ethic infused with bounds of energy. In her first placement she was thrown in at the deep end and had to learn on the go, but came up trumps.

Sammi, he was a lovely quiet chap with two young children and an electric scooter, that didn't go fast but took him for miles. He was a religious person and was always reflective. Sammi was always carrying more than he could handle. You almost wanted to follow him and scoop below to catch any falling papers before they reached the ground. He was easy to work with and in my first placement, I worked with him in the same school. Learning how to juggle our work during the busy school day.

Kajal, she was highly driven, maybe because of her Indian background and the fact she went to a grammar school too. She had high standards and her subject knowledge was solid. Kajal was a single mother which kept her extremely focused, especially during those long days and sleepless nights preparing lesson plans and completing assignments. On top of that she also had to organise her daughter's schedule as well.

Eno, she specialized in Science, so we did not have our sessions together. We became firm friends and would often go home together in the evenings excited at the prospect of becoming qualified teachers. She was a solid black woman with three kids, so did not have time for nonsense!

She had a positive aura about her and was so focused towards achieving her goals. We encouraged each other, laughing and crying along the way. We would swap tales of our experiences in schools and 'Having to bite our tongues', knowing once we qualified all would be well.

Doulth was the man. He had a gentle heart and was always willing to help out, even though he was finding the course tricky. Doulth was married with two young kids and just wanted them to have a secure future with their dad earning a reasonable wage and being confident about his future employment. The school holidays would have enabled him to spend time with them, which is what he really wanted, having a good 'work/life balance'.

Ademola was my brilliant brother from another mother. Standing together both of us looked similar with my low hair cut matching his and our clothes sense coordinating. He was a 'Super Malt' lover (which is a delicious, refreshing beverage from Nigeria) – what more can I say?

We all enjoyed working with each other and tried to support one another with lesson planning and advice on the various hilarious situations we found ourselves in within the schools we were doing our placements. We were constantly tired and mentally drained, but we pushed on towards our goals, knowing once we qualified everything would be great. So much enthusiasm we had, we just could not wait to get in front of the classroom. Our mission was to teach and make sure every student learnt and were blown away with our lessons that we planned for hours. We were going to change the world!

We heard that approximately 30-50% of new teachers leave the profession after five years. We couldn't believe it! I remember telling Eno, teaching my subject is all I wanted to do, I can't imagine ever wanting to leave!

I remember having to team teach with a fellow student teacher, a lesson right at the beginning of my training in Sarah Imbrush's school. Can you imagine? The pressure! Anyway, I went round to her house, we planned the content, because we were team teaching, we also planned who was going to talk and how we were going to deliver the lesson, also where we both would stand in the room. How we would give the students instructions and how we would model the way we wanted the answers to be presented. How we would differentiate the work for the most-able to the least. We had it all down to a tee, our PowerPoint had things flying in from all directions in various bright colours. We even had extension questions for the more eager students. It took us ALL day to plan that one lesson, me leaving her house in the early hours of the morning.

The day came. We were both in our correct positions, with the students about to commence on the worksheet. The topic was 'Drawing linear graphs'. As they started, some student piped up that there was not enough space to draw the axis on the Maths paper we had given them (big squares, instead of the little ones); this was soon followed by another student. We quickly looked at one another, then the question, then it slowly dawned on us, that indeed this was the case; from then on it was downhill as we hadn't planned for this. Both of us trying to resolve the problem but confusing the students more. Don't ask me how but we survived until the end of the lesson, I think by changing the parameters and improvising?

On reflection, it was clear that because we hadn't actually done any of the questions that we had given to the students, we just presumed that providing the questions and having the answers was enough, which Sarah said you must never do. She explained that we need to foresee what the students might struggle with and plan our lessons that way. We were both so disappointed with our performance, it really was a lesson learned for both of us.

As well as the teaching, we learnt a lot of theory behind education and the different learning styles of learning through different books like *'The Elephant in the classroom'* by Jo Boaler or *'How to be an amazing teacher'* by Caroline Bentley-Davis, also *'Learning and Teaching'* by Viv Ellis, just to name a few. We also learnt about various special needs, like Autism, Asperger Syndrome, ADHD etc. and the best way to teach those students. I lapped it all up.

I often wondered why Filomena had picked me. I got the chance to ask her a few weeks later, once we had settled into the course.

Me: Can I ask you, why you choose me, Filomena, I am still trying to get my head around it?

Filomena: Why would you ask that, Shola; don't you believe in yourself?

Me: Well...

Filomena: Remember in the interview I asked you about the course that you did at Birkbeck?

Me: Yes.

Filomena: That was what singled you out, we on the panel thought it must have been hard for you to return to education in your thirties while being fully employed. Therefore, we figured you must have been driven and be able to apply yourself, which is what is needed for this course.

Me: Oh... I thought, if only you knew...

Filomena: We knew we had to have you, Shola.

Blushing, I said in reply,

Me: Oh...really... thanks, Filomena! Wow, I thought, who would have thought an evening class, that put a dent in my bank account would have been my saving grace!

Assignment galore

During the early stages of the course, we were inundated with assignments and projects and all had to be presented in a typed format, submitted online – my worst nightmare! I didn't own a computer, so I would spend hours in my local internet shop trying to focus amidst the smell of freshly sliced kebabs drifting in each time the door opened, which was frequently. People trooping in and out combined with armpit sweat and the constant loud chatter of people who were paying for phone calls to loved ones far away. This was really a tough environment to concentrate, but I simply had no other choice.

"Headphones in, scarf around your mouth, focus, Shola, you have a deadline!"

One particular assignment, I was already late by a day. I had been chucked out of the shop. The shopkeeper could not leave the shop open any longer. He would normally close at 9pm, but stayed open till 10pm for me; he had to go home to his family, no matter how much I begged him to stay open longer.

When Filomena heard about my late submission, she called me in for a late evening meeting. I was worried as I did not know what she would say.

Me: Am I getting kicked off the course? I said in one breath.

She simply replied,

Filomena: Why was your assignment late?

I went into the situation with the computer and my reliance on the internet café aka kebab shop.

Me: I am so sorry; I am trying to be more organised...

I had my head down, with my fingers crossed, praying please don't kick me off the course, please don't kick me off the course!

Filomena: That's not good enough, Shola...

I really did not want to disappoint her, I needed to let her know that I was doing my best and totally committed to the course. Then she said something that nearly made me fall off my chair.

Filomena: I have arranged for you to have a computer for the remainder of the course, if that is ok with you?

Me: What? Are you sure? That would be bloody fantastic!

I thought, "You mean I do not have to go back to that stinky place?" I was in so much shock, that she would do that for me. It meant that I could work from the luxury of my own home, at my own pace, not at the internet shop's opening and closing times, but whenever I wanted, what a Godsend!

After that my assignments were never late again and the quality of my work was so much better. If I hadn't got the computer, there would have been a high chance that I would have flunked the course. Filomena was not having that happen to me on her watch – totally outstanding support!

TUESDAY JUNE 16TH 2020

Primary school observations

As part of the course, we as trainee teachers were sent into a primary school to see how the children learn, especially in Year 6 (the last year of primary school). We had to organise our own primary school placement. I was lucky enough to be on talking terms with an inspirational black head teacher of the local primary school. My nephew Seun had gone there and had fond memories of her. She supported me in making it happen, welcoming me into her school, big up Ms Jackson!

The school was rated 'Good' by Ofsted and I was allowed to shadow an excellent teacher called Marian and observe her good teaching practice. How she communicated with her class, with the parents and most importantly how she juggled all the tasks required of her, within the school day.

I often wondered how Ms Jackson, a woman of colour, managed to be in that role for nearly 20 years. The answer was: go pass the school early in the morning and late in the evening, she would always be there, in her office working her socks off. Ms Jackson was definitely on top of things, plus she had a fantastic, trusted and loyal support team behind her from what I have observed.

She relayed a story once about a typical scenario.

Ms Jackson: "My deputy is white and when we have visitors come into the school, if I am standing next to my Deputy, they will always assume that she is the head teacher. When we correct them, they are always extremely apologetic and... embarrassed!"

She ran a tight ship. It was a real eye opener for me having that experience, right then I said I could never work in a primary school. You had to be super-organised and be able to cater to all those little children, who at that age can be quite clingy. Also, you needed to have so much energy, it was absolutely exhausting! I could not deal with all that movement; one minute the child was there next minute they were gone!

Being in a primary school the kids generally have only ONE teacher for all their lessons and stay in the same room for the whole of the day. Apart from assemblies, break, lunch times and of course PE. It's a total change for them to adjust to secondary school as they have to move from room to room, teacher to teacher, and lesson to lesson. It was important for us, as teaching professionals in secondary school, to understand that transition and try to make it as smooth and easy for the kids as possible.

Parents' Evening – Grammar school style

We as the trainee teachers were to attend Year 9's parents' evening to support Sarah and the school and also to observe how things should be done.

She had arranged Maths activities for the students, in-between the parents seeing teachers, like a kind of workshop. We were to usher them into groups and supervise. At 7pm when the doors opened, I had never seen anything like it: an avalanche of parents, grandparents, aunties, uncles, sisters, brothers, Godparents; it seemed everybody was there that evening. We pulled up extra chairs to accommodate the families; all they were interested in was their child's predicted grades and ways in which to improve them. The child was simply the centre of everything and you could visibly see it, which is powerful. Every single child had a flock, no exceptions!

Looking back at that and comparing it to the parents' evenings that I have had since, over the years, the students that you desperately need to reach, the parents don't attend. In some cases, for legitimate reasons like work commitments, other children and time constraints.

TUESDAY JUNE 16TH 2020

But some parents, sorry to say, just can't be bothered, which is so sad! I would even chase up parents to give them alternative times and days that worked for them. After a while experience tells you the ones who want to be part of their child's education and engage with the school system and those who just don't and do everything to avoid your calls.

***

I remember just before I started my first placement, I had a one-to-one session with Filomena. She raised a really important issue.

Filomena: You trust me now, don't you, Shola?

Me: Of course, Filomena,

answering, quite puzzled.

Filomena: I have noticed that you wear a lot of dark clothes.

As much as I was fond of this woman, was she dissing my outfits?

Me: Hmm... I have never really thought about it.

Filomena: You seem to possess lots of tops and bottoms that happen to be dark.

Me: Really??

Filomena: Can you imagine standing in front of a class, what feelings do you want to invoke in your students?

> **Me:** Happy, joyful and interested?

I said, really having to think about it.

> **Filomena**: I would like you to make a conscious effort to throw in a splash of colour in your attire. Maybe do it by adding some bright accessories, making those small changes can positively affect you and your students mentally. Try it and let me know.

I had never really thought about it. When I went back home and checked my wardrobe, I realised a majority of my clothes where indeed BLACK! Filomena was right, how did she observe that? I asked myself.

Black tops and shiny black blouses, black matt trousers, skinny, wide bottoms, black cardigans and jumpers, black shoes and boots, even my socks were black! This was ridiculous! So I had to make the effort and find the time to buy brighter items, especially as I would be in front of a class, independently, very soon.

New site – September 2010

During the time I was at Rokeby school, there was talk over the years of the refurbishment of the school buildings through the *'Newham's Building Schools for The Future programme'*. There was quite a bit of land surrounding the school and with some imagination it could have really been a fantastic opportunity to create something beautiful and remain on the site that the school had been on for over half a century!

We were told the space was needed for the Olympics and the school would eventually be broken down to accommodate this lifetime event. It turned from refurbishing the buildings into moving the school onto a new site in Canning Town and building it up from scratch with the doors opening in September 2010. My opinion was,

I wanted the school to remain where it was so the students could properly be part of the regeneration of Stratford and be involved in London Olympics 2012 as a lot of the local schools were doing.

I remember the recruitment had started for youth ambassadors from the immediate local schools a few years before. I thought it would be a fantastic opportunity for the boys to volunteer their services and they also were excited about the prospect of being involved in this historic event.

There was plenty of space to build up or outwards on the present school site. Instead, the decision was made and the school was built right on a busy main road with guess-who for neighbours? – a bloody McDonalds! I couldn't believe what I was witnessing!

And we claim to care for our children's health. How can the kids resist such temptations every single day? How was a child supposed to concentrate on learning with the smell of Big Macs every day drifting through the class windows, especially if they were already hungry? Anyway, rant over…

Oh, yeah, as they say in my country, *"I am sure a lot of handshakes and winks were made oh!"*, for anyone to place a school next to any type of fast-food venue is ludicrous! How do we expect the students to keep healthy, walking back and forth from that establishment daily? I am sure a few years back, fast-food outlets were not allowed to open close to any schools, but yet this woman thought it was a great idea to plonk her school right next to one!

What's upsetting is that the old school was given a new name and kept as a school till this very day with roughly the same number of students, go figure! Rant over this time, I promise!

Friends

To be honest, I was a shit friend. My poor friends from secondary school suffered during the years I was intertwined with the grievance and the court procedures. Every time I would meet up with them, that's all I could talk about, Charlotte this, Charlotte that. At the start they were really understanding:

"She did what??"

"She said that…oh really!"

But after a while I could see that as soon as I went into a recent development with my case, their faces would just cloud over and I could see I had lost them.

I imagined that they were thinking:

"When is she ever gonna get over this, can she please for God's sake talk about something else! Anything other than this bloody woman that we don't even know!"

One specific occasion it was my birthday. My friends had arranged a surprise birthday dinner; we were all to meet in a Nigerian restaurant called *Enish* in South London. There were glorious, massive helium-coloured balloons, a beautiful cake and plenty of *Orijin*, which is a local alcoholic Nigerian beverage, easy to drink, but lethal if you try to get up and walk. Anyway, I was tipsy and someone mistakably asked me about how far my case had come.

"Well…" I went into great depths of the court case, at the same time my spirit seemed to leave the table and float from above. I could see myself talking without taking a breather and getting more and more animated and riled up with the unfairness of the situation. I looked over at each of my friends and saw the pain in their eyes, mostly because they could not help me. I saw the beautiful balloons and presents and the effort each of them had made to come to celebrate this special day with me, and at that moment I realised that this was taking over my life.

I had subjected them to this spur of rubbish that wasn't really important after all, in the great scheme of things they each had their own problems. All they were trying to do was have a good time with me. My bestie saw the mood change and saved the day by bursting a rude joke about the way the pounded yam was presented on the plate and we all burst out laughing, then she smoothly moved the conversation on from there.

I looked over at her and said 'Thank you!' with my eyes. I made the conscious decision there and then to not let this woman take over my life anymore and upset my relationships with my closest friends. I felt I had changed during this whole Charlotte aka Stone issue, a part of my life had been lost that I could never get back and I had forgotten how to be a friend.

Representation

Bless Sabrina, she took my case on pro bono to her firm as my union was unresponsive. We had also put in a claim for 'Constructive Dismissal'. She prepared all the paperwork and corresponded with the respondents and tribunal, letting me know what was happening at each stage. We received the respondents' reply on the ET3 form, they had contested all the points I raised, surprise surprise! So we were definitely going forward to tribunal.

Unfortunately, Sabrina had to leave the firm after a few months. Thankfully, I was passed on to a lovely African women called Wonta, who attended a 'Case Management' meeting with me on the 5th of October 2010 held at the East London Employment Tribunal. In the meeting we had to clarify any issues, submit schedule of losses, agree which witnesses to be called and any remaining documentation that needed to be disclosed.

We also had to provide dates that both parties would be free. The nearest date was the summer of the following year; I couldn't believe it was taking so long!

We were interested in judicial mediation; I think that involved ACAS but we never heard back from the respondents, unfortunately.

First Placement – November 2010

I wanted to look sharp, so I went to the barbers, so they could give me a good fade. It was actually hard work, keeping a short haircut. You could not afford to let it go, carrying a brush with me everywhere I went, otherwise I would have looked like someone who 'Had just stepped off the boat'!

After a while we were let out on our own. Working in schools, reading and abiding by their policies. Learning how to plan lessons, modelling good practice to the students, observing teaching styles, writing schemes of work for year groups, marking and planning assessments, giving and collecting homework and generally being able to cope with a timetable. Even though, as a trainee teacher, your timetable was reduced slightly to give you time to complete all your administration and believe me even with that, there was never enough time. Sammi and I were one of the first to arrive at school and the last to leave – bless the long-suffering caretaker of that school!

This mixed school in Southend was a culture shock for me. I was teaching mainly white children, who were disrespectful and swore directly at me and gave me the impression that they couldn't care less about me, talk less of education. They were nice enough, until you asked them to do something. It seemed that they had other priorities, especially the girls. It was the first time I saw girls with such short skirts, pushing them way above the knees, exposing too much skin, as far as I was concerned.

Wearing so much makeup and regularly pouting their lips in their pocket mirrors or applying full scale foundation in my lessons, I couldn't believe what I was seeing! You were not allowed to seize anything from them, which was my first instinct, so you would politely tell them to put it away, and that task could take them all lesson. It made my blood boil, and they knew it!

The evidence of makeup would be everywhere, on their blouses, blazers, hands and even on their exercise books. What made me mad, and most importantly, is that it took focus away from the lesson and their learning, which was my primary concern.

I think back to my secondary school days in Nigeria, where even thinking about makeup was an absolute luxury. We were too busy trying to please our parents by focusing on our education…such different times!

I remember saying to one of the regular teachers:

"Is there no school rule about this makeup thing, it's too much!"

"A lot of the girls have low self-esteem, so use makeup to boost confidence," he said.

Oh that makes sense, I thought – at that age, peer approval is so important, especially in this day of social media, but I still found hard to understand, really.

I must say, I remember being quite sad about this. I wanted to start a campaign to promote self-worth. I wanted to get role models in to talk to the girls. I wanted to have self-esteem workshops. I wanted to do so much for those girls, but then I realised I was not there to change the world. I was there to follow the school policies and that was not the school's priority at the time.

I was there to try to pass my teacher training. "Stay focused, Shola!" I kept telling myself, I could not afford to rub anyone up the wrong way, especially Senior Management.

I did try to talk one-on-one with some girls, but they took offence straight away.

"You don't need to wear so much makeup, you are beautiful as you are," I said to them.

"What do you mean, Miss, are you taking the piss?" they would reply in shock and embarrassment.

Cringing with the swear word, I did my best to ignore it and said, "No, it's just not good for your skin, it blocks the pores," trying to make them see sense from a different angle.

"Are you saying I should come to school without makeup?" they would reply back in horror.

"Maybe think of reducing the amount," I would say in defence, hoping they would take some time to think about it and know I was coming from a good place. Some of those girls needed help and didn't realise it then. Unfortunately, I was only there for a short time.

Oh Oh!

I remember in that placement, a complaint had come in about me from one of the students and I was summoned by the Head of Year, after school.

> **HOY:** Linda was upset about how you approached her about her late homework.

I remembered vaguely speaking to her about the homework task I had given one of my classes, hers was missing and I had simply asked for it.

> **HOY:** She did not know your name, she identified you by saying 'The big, black bald-headed bitch' as he coughed and looked down at the notepad.

I couldn't stop myself from laughing. "What a creative description of me, she will go far in life!"

I thought, really, are you not going to sanction her for using that type of language about a member of staff? Even if I was only temporary. His only concern was that I was not too heavy on the deadline for the homework given.

HOY: Some students have personal problems and homework is not really their priority.

I thought to myself in frustration, but she's got no problem opening her mouth to abuse people who are here to help her, imagine! So disrespectful! How can we expect results from these students if we are allowing them to feel so confident and bold to say that to a senior member of staff about another member of staff, without any form of reprimand? I would not accept that type of language from a student about anyone I worked with, period!

I bit my tongue, breathed in deeply and calmly said:

Me: No problem, Sir, I will give her an extension until next week.

Looking back now, I can try to understand where the HOY was coming from. Indeed, some students had other priorities, not by choice, but their education needed to be a top priority and that just didn't seem to be the case. Guess what, I never ever did receive the homework from that student!

***

All in all, I enjoyed this placement. I could not have asked for any more support from the Maths department and the school in general. I even got invited to Lisa's wedding, the Maths department's administrative lady. Anytime I hear Adele *'Make you feel my love'* I remember seeing the joy and happiness in her eyes and the love between her and her partner. Unfortunately, we have not kept in touch as I would have liked, which I notice happens when you change schools. It's like living with a family and then moving out and in with another, being swept up with trying to fit in and finding your niche in the new school. By the time you have settled in, time passes and it gets more and more difficult to reconnect with your old family, because you don't really seem to have anything more in common or the time to invest in those relationships anymore … sadly.

Second Placement – January 2011

We had to sort out our individual second placements. Some of my fellow trainees had to write to schools to ask them whether they could do their placements there. The schools got some funding for doing this, but it was still a commitment, plus plenty of paperwork. Many schools just did not want to go out on a limb for someone they didn't know, so there was a lot of replies, which boiled down to NO!

"Sorry we can't assist you with this matter."

"We don't have sufficient classes for you to teach."

"You should have got in touch at the beginning of the academic year."

Sad to say, apart from Kajal, it was only the teachers of colour left on the shelf, with all the will in the world Filomena could not find us placements. It was critical we got into two schools, otherwise we would not be able to qualify that year. We were advised to try to find our own placements as time was running out. I could not believe it!

Luckily, dear Jenny "Dreads" from the Birkbeck course said I could come to Tower Hamlets in East London, which was a stone's throw from Stratford to do my training with her at her school. I cannot explain how grateful I was to her that I didn't have to go through what my fellow colleagues went through, desperately looking for a school that would take them.

Tower Hamlets was one of the poorest boroughs in London and just next to Newham, my borough. It was in the shadow of Canary Wharf, an extension of the City, with its exclusive financial deals happening daily in expensive surroundings. It was not easy for the students living next door in poverty, but the students used that to focus on what could be possible if they worked hard.

By now, I was more confident in the classroom. I really enjoyed this school, there were a high percentage of Black and Ethnic minority children here. I found the students worked well and really wanted to be achievers, plus there was ample support from the parents, and no one swore at me, at least not to my face!

The Head of Maths was a tall, attractive, intelligent light-skinned Jamaican gentleman called Andrew. He was reflective person and always ready to support and give you constructive feedback. I found working there felt like a breeze – all I had to do was concentrate on my lesson plans and how to convey what I had to teach to the students. With Dreads giving me advice and me able to shadow her in her tutor group and in her lessons, I found it an eye opener watching her as she built relationships on trust with the students and how she taught her lessons with such ease. I hoped to be able to do that one day.

I was also able to observe Andrew and the rest of the Maths department and their different styles of teaching and see how they used student data to write assessments and improve how they delivered their lessons. I picked up so many tips that I still use today in my lesson planning.

What a contrast in schools!

I count myself to be really lucky. At least two other black ladies didn't get their second placement in a school. The last time I heard, they had to do the year again and who knows they might end up in the same situation again!

Back to my case...

Wonta continued to represent me. I met her a few times to prepare my case but as we were nearing the hearing, she said she would only be able to assist me with negotiations to settle, but funding could not stretch to representing me at court. Bottom line was, I would have to do it myself!

I thought about representing myself, but how was I to investigate? I kept hearing that famous saying:

'Anyone who represents themselves is a fool' – I can understand that because you can become so emotional with your own case and unable to be objective to the witnesses, when being cross-examined. I knew I fell into that category.

For example, if I was to question Charlotte aka Stone, I don't know whether I would be able to hold myself back! Also, I was a *'nobody'* – when I called the centre that was holding the TA courses to find out more information, they refused to answer any of my questions and literally put the phone down on me! Can you imagine!

I asked around frantically about legal representation at short notice. Some friends recommended a man named Leonard; he had experience of employment law. We had a brief conversation about my case and agreed that we should meet.

Could Leonard step in at such short notice? My fingers and toes were crossed!

It all boiled down to this meeting – could I convince him to take my case? We were meeting in a café near Finsbury Park station in North London. I wanted to get there with plenty of time to spare, as I am very organised like that, but maybe because of the importance of the meeting, I think I was subconsciously stressed. I arrived at the station, but came out of the wrong bloody entrance!

I was flustered by the time I finally reached him on the other side of the station. Thankfully, he was patiently sitting down in the cafe, having ordered some type of beverage already. Breathe, Shola, breathe… I could now tell my story without being in floods of tears.

I waited to hear what his thoughts were; I have no money; would he take my case? It wasn't about believing in my case, it was whether I had a fair chance of winning in court! Indeed, he did, he said I had a high probability of winning and seamlessly took on my case. Leonard began in earnest finding relevant case law and preparing my case for the upcoming employment tribunal.

The anxiety was tremendous all through this process. Firstly, thinking the union would represent me and then getting let down. Then one minute I have Sabrina, the next she's gone. Then Wonta, who then pulled out at the last minute because of financial issues. Finally, now putting all my hope in Leonard, a light at the end of the tunnel. What a bloody nightmare, that I shouldn't have had to have gone through!

At least now I have got representation at my employment tribunal. Thank you, God!

Friday June 19th 2020

Today was *'Juneteenth'*. I had never heard of event this before, most probably because I don't live in the States, but with heightened feelings, there was a strong focus on the celebrations this year.

A lot of African Americans have claimed this day as their Independence Day instead of the 4th of July. It commemorates the day in 1865 when slaved people of Texas were freed, so technically celebrated the end of slavery in the United States. This day is also known as 'Freedom Day', which makes sense. It is a recognised paid holiday in Texas, but people are pushing for it to be a national holiday for all.

It was fantastic for me to witness this celebration on the different news channels – the fact that a day that was important to the black community was shown on mainstream TV, just shows we are moving in the right direction.

***

I jam to Beyoncé's tunes. That girl knows how to move but more importantly she is a business woman and knows what sells, that's why she is so successful. Beyoncé's new song *'Black Parade'* was released today, a celebration of black culture, heritage and excellence. The sound is quite gritty, but catchy and reminds me of Africa.

The proceeds will go to her BeyGOOD's Black Business Impact Fund which supports Black-owned small businesses in need. Can you imagine, getting help from Beyoncé's organisation, she is assisting her own, so inspiring!

She also launched *'a directory of black-owned businesses'* which solely features black-owned businesses across the country. She is not just talking the talk, she is walking the walk; Beyoncé crosses all colour barriers, so this is a massive deal for those small business to reach another level with the publicity they will receive being on this list.

***

Back in the UK, on Wednesday 17th of June, the governors of Oxford University College voted for the removal of the controversial statue of Cecil Rhodes. They said, *"After a thoughtful period of debate and reflection"* – and in *"full awareness of the impact these decisions are likely to have in Britain and around the world"*, hopefully he will be placed in a museum in the near future, where we can all learn about him in context.

I personally was happy that this decision was made. If I attended that college I would not want to look up to that kind of person literally, especially now knowing what his background was. Would this decision have been made, if all those protesters had not demanded it?

Witnesses

At the time when all this was happening to me, a lot of the people who were employed by the school, people of colour and even white people were absolutely horrified, some who witnessed some of the incidents said to me:

Potential Witness: Gosh, what you are going through is terrible, Shola!

Me: Thanks, building my case now, would you be able to be a witness for me?

Potential Witness: Sure thing, Shola, whatever you need, just let me know.

I had this conversation with several people and felt at least I had support from them. Remember I had been to their houses, knew names of their pets, surely they had my back!

As we received confirmation of the date of the tribunal, I contacted some of the supposed witnesses to let them know.

Potential Witness: I've been thinking about it, am sorry, Shola, I just can't do it!

Me: Why not? I really need you!

Potential Witness: I can't risk losing my job.

Me: We need to come together; we need to show everyone that Charlotte was wrong!

Potential Witness: Hmmm, not sure about that. I am sure you understand I have a family to feed...

Me: Really! What can I say? You do what you have to do...

As I put the phone down, I understood what their dilemma was, would I do it myself? If I was in that situation and this happened to a fellow colleague, the question would be, how would I feel if I didn't do it?

Another potential witness:

FRIDAY JUNE 19TH 2020

Potential witness: You mean I can't do it anonymously; I would actually have to stand up in court?

Me: Yes, most probably, especially if you have written a statement (I was not gonna lie to them).

Potential witness: In that case, I don't think I can do it.

Me: Maybe you could just come along to support me.

A pause.

Potential witness: I don't think that will be possible either...

Me: Really, that's such a shame...

Cherelle, the other Cover supervisor was still on the fence. She really could not afford to lose her job, even though she knew what she was going on was so wrong.

In the end the only person who was happy to stand by me from the school was Debbie, even though the possibility of her losing her job was extremely high. I said to her on several occasions:

Me: Are you sure, Debs?

Debbie: I am not going to lie on the stand, Shola, I will answer truthfully and tell it like it is...

Me: But you still have to work there though!

Debbie: I know, but I witnessed some of this behaviour, I have to say something...

Me: Thank you, but I am still worried about you.

Debbie: Don't worry about me, I am a strong person.

And indeed, she was, she stuck to her word and stood by me throughout the process.

Dr Ju and Julie despite their own disabilities were willing to write statements about my character and work ethic, also attend court if needed. I wanted that to be a last option – after all, I was not on trial!

It took a lot for people with disabilities just to be able to live a normal life, without having the pressure and drama of trying to get to court for one of their ex-workers. They assured me they were up for it, but I was not convinced. It wasn't their battle, after all, they had helped and supported me in more ways than they could ever imagine during this case, without having to physically be in the court.

Ofsted – May 2011

I did not find out about the timing of this visit until I was writing this book – I could not believe this had happened just before my tribunal took place in August of that year.

I thought one of the roles of Ofsted was to look at the management of a school. They do in relation to the children, but not at staff disputes with the Head teacher. In my opinion all grievances listed for tribunal should trigger something to inform Ofsted or the DfE (Department for Education). Somewhere, somehow surely someone should have raised this issue while going through the paperwork, especially as it has to do with the performance of management and leadership ultimately and who was paying for all their damn lawyers and barristers??

Ofsted should not give ratings to schools when a tribunal is lodged; in my case, it was common knowledge from the previous year.

It would be an incentive for schools not to have any grievances or to resolve them before tribunal stage. The school was visited in March and the report published in May, graded the school 'Outstanding'. Can you imagine?

'The motivational and committed head teacher, along with a highly skilled leadership team' was one of the quotes from the report, motivational! Really? By treating people unfairly. I wonder whether she will engrave that sentence on her tombstone, it just makes me feel like throwing up!

How can this be so with a discrimination case just about to take place against the school in a few months' time, what if the judgement had gone the other way? In my opinion when a tribunal against a school is logged, Ofsted should delay their visit until after the judgment.

I would not want to send my child to a school that got "Outstanding" from Ofsted to later find out that they were actually found guilty of discriminating against their staff. It really does not sit well with me at all, I don't think the parents would have been impressed either.

Tribunal – August 2011

Finally, the day had come where my story would be told. If people knew what had happened to me, of course they would say it was not fair. How could any logical person not come to that conclusion?

The tribunal had listed my case for five days. I didn't know at the time it would be extended for another three days in September, because of the sheer amount of evidence. I arrived early at East India station wearing my church clothes and good shoes. It was so close to the money and decision makers in Canary Wharf, thank God I looked smart. Even though I felt really nervous, I was hopeful. It was more than two years now, since I had had to resign. Was I really going to get some justice finally? As I went down the steep, long stairs, my knees felt wobbly. I looked across at the intimidating building where I would be for the next few days.

Everyone looked to have a purpose around here. Dashing around were extremely well-dressed individuals carrying briefcases or with thick shoulder bags brimming with papers. Some had the convenience of having a small suitcase with wheels, like a trolley, pulling it along behind them as they talked frantically on the phone. It all seemed quite busy and overwhelming. There was a queue for the coffee van, but I was not ready to consume any more caffeine, my nerves didn't need any more stimulation.

We had arrived in plenty of time, just in case I needed to go over last-minute stuff with Leonard. Bless him, he always looked smart and his shoes sparkled with shine. It was intimidating going into court, me and my small faithful group and the other side with their masses of people, advisors and lawyers. Carrying bundles of paper all talking to one another under their breath, looking really smart and important. Of course, Charlotte aka Stone was there with her trusted ally by her side, Tom Alexander.

Walking into the room we would be based in for the hearing, my heart was beating. We stood up and waited for the three people on the panel to walk in and then we sat down.

There were two white men and a white woman; my instinctive thought was, were they really going to understand my case? Could they really relate? Would they be as shocked as me about my treatment?

We only really heard from the main judge, Judge Prichard, who sat in the middle. The others would whisper any concerns that they had and he in turn would voice them to us.

In response to Leonard's concerns about Debbie being a witness, Judge Prichard said sternly somewhere at the start of the proceedings.

FRIDAY JUNE 19TH 2020

"I want it to be noted, that anyone who has decided to stand as a witness for the Claimant from the school should not be victimized if they choose to continue working at the school."

We could have summoned our other witnesses, but we didn't want them to come if they were not happy to attend and give their testimony. We had to summon Debbie to confirm and be questioned on her statement, which she was happy to do and did it impeccably; even Judge Prichard was impressed with her.

Thankfully, Cherelle came around and did the right thing, just in time. She was very nervous about giving evidence, but bless her, she really just told it as it was.

When I was cross-examined by their lawyers, it was gruelling!

They stayed clear from the main issues like the TA course and my lack of career progression. They could not find anything about the quality of my work or my character. Saying all along that my motives were wanting to become a teacher. It truly felt I was the one on trial, like I had done something wrong for asking for equal treatment.

I could only doodle on my paper while the witnesses from the other side were being questioned by Leonard, obviously avoiding eye contact with me. Inside I was boiling and just wanted to lash out at them to tell the truth, for crying out loud!

Can you imagine who they called as a witness? Grant aka Pastor!

When he spoke and answered questions, all I could see was his mouth moving, but I couldn't hear what he was saying. All I could think of was the many times I had supported him over the years. When I asked him to support me in the teacher training, he didn't and now in court, he was stabbing me in the back. I was so disappointed with him as a person, a pastor and as a black man.

Even Tom Alexander had submitted a statement which clearly stated whose side he was on in his capacity as the Principal Human Resources Officer for Newham. Another black man who I went to for help in my desperate hour and spoke to in confidence, turned around and stabbed me in the back too.

Seeing Charlotte aka Stone being questioned was the first time I saw her unnerved. Her explanations were thin on the ground; you could see she was not comfortable with being asked to expand on her decisions.

At some point in time Judge Prichard said,

"If it walks like a duck, looks like a duck, then…"

There was laughter in the room on both sides, you just don't expect the judge to be busting jokes. I had never heard this saying before, so I did not know what he meant. It was later Hubby explained it to me and I understood what the Judge was saying in-between the lines.

It was painful watching the response from the other side as they were questioned by the judge over and over. It was embarrassing that they could not recall facts and could not back decisions that they had made during the time I was employed there. The judge and panel simply did not understand their thinking.

On one occasion when he questioned one of the governors, Ted Sparrowhawk, on the stand:

Judge P: So, did you undertake any investigation?

TS: No.

Judge P: Why ever not?

TS: There was no evidence to investigate.

He said that last sentence with so much confidence and no shame, there were gasps all around, we all looked at each other, can you believe this? We said to each other with our eyes.

"Look at all the evidence in front of you!" Judge Prichard said to him, frustratingly pointing to the bundle, which included all of the letters, witnesses, examples of incidents, minutes of meetings, contract etc. all in the chunky folders.

I was actually shocked that someone in his position would confidently say that for all to hear. Surely he didn't really believe in what he was saying. It all became clear now, his behaviour at the grievance appeal meeting, when I received the response, the day after the meeting. In his opinion no investigation needed to take place, so my question is, how did they all come to the appeal decision without looking at any of the evidence?

Last day!

At the end of the hearing, some drama occurred with the other side submitting some evidence at the last minute to the panel in the middle of our submissions. It was a document about my Comparator – Daniel aka Lazy. It showed that they had indeed backdated his pay, which was not their intention. Leonard commented on this and said this was an example of less favourable treatment and the Judge and panel agreed.

As proceedings were brought to a close, Judge Prichard ruled partly in my favour unsurprisingly, for all to hear. We were overjoyed, I was overjoyed! Finally, someone had seen through the bullshit and had done the right thing! We all went for a celebratory drink at the local bar. We were happy the case was over and it had gone in our favour. We could not wait to get the written formal confirmation and finally putting this damn nightmare behind us!

Back to school

Meanwhile at the end of the teacher training, Emma got a job straight away in her local area, Cerys got a job from her first placement, think she was put second in charge in the Maths department. Kajal was the only person of colour to get a role and she had to uproot and move all the way to West London, even though she had a child. I really admired her, she was so focused and driven, even though she had an accent this did not stop her; in fact, she used it to show, she was proud of her heritage and confident of her approach. I am sure she is most probably Head of a Maths department now, if not Senior Management, she had that much potential!

Doulth kind of dropped out before we finished, it was such a shame as he invested so much time and energy into the course. The financial help was not enough for him to support his family and pay his bills. He was going to pick it up again the following year while he saved and took up a job to allow him to keep himself out of the red.

Ademola decided to take a year out and study something supplementary to his teacher training so he could be a better asset to any establishment he decided to work for in the future. I thought what a loss to the teaching profession!

Tuition

As for me, once I qualified and had Qualified Teachers Status (QTS), I started applying for Maths teaching roles. In the meantime, I started to do private tuition. Eno had been doing it for a while and really encouraged me to try it, to build up my experience and develop my teaching style.

It was word of mouth really, getting my first clients, but as news got around, I started getting more and more calls. I could have easily done this full-time, but I wanted to work within schools and get more experience.

I think I was more nervous than the students, when I first started, because what I really wanted was them to perform well back in their classes with their teachers. The feedback I got from parents attending parent evenings was that their children had become more confident and made significant progress since they started one-on-one tuition with me. So you can imagine that the parents wanted the private lessons to continue, but I had to make that decision to wean myself off them so I could concentrate on getting more experience in a school setting.

Initial teaching work

I knew I could not work for any of the schools within London borough of Newham. That woman, Charlotte aka Stone, had too much influence!

I was not going to risk my career on what that woman would say to anyone asking for a reference. It was illegal to give a 'bad reference', but I was still not taking any chances. I heard from the grapevine that after giving a written reference, Stone would follow it up with a telephone call to give a verbal reference – you can imagine, both references would not be similar. I made the decision early on in my teaching career not to ask Stone for a reference or work within the schools in the London borough of Newham.

I remember making the mistake of applying for an HLTA (Higher Learning Teacher Assistant) role in Newham before I did the teacher's training, I aced the interview and near enough was given the role on condition of acceptable references. The panel looked optimistic and generally happy to be having me as part of the team, but after a few days, I received a call from the school and the tone was completely different. All of a sudden, they were not able to take my application any further and they could not be specific about the reasons why they had had a change of heart. I vowed never to use Charlotte aka Stone again for a reference and Thank God I never have!

What no one said to me, or maybe I just didn't hear, was that even though you are qualified to teach a specific subject, if you work in a school, the school can ask you to teach ANY subject. If you refuse you could be out of a job and this goes for agency work too. You are employed as a teacher first, unless the school asks for a specific subject teacher.

I joined an agency outside the borough of Newham. One of the first roles, thankfully, was covering a Maths teacher for a few days as she was unwell. It was a girls' school in the middle of Central London. I remember thinking I love these kind of old buildings where bits have been added. The architect had to be imaginative as the site was so small. The school had a small playground, but no green to play on. How can you not have a playing field with real grass in a school?

I think back to my old secondary school in Chingford in East London with lots of green space for us to enjoy and proper oxygen from all the trees around. The girls at this school did not seem bothered. I am sure they went to the second family home at weekends in the country with acres of land or holiday trips far and wide. At least the students had the possibility of having that in the future with the kind of wages they would be able to demand. Let's be honest, no one was failing in this type of school!

It was a total breeze. I gave them the work supplied and they just got on with it. The girls were so polite and respectful; they had been grilled on the importance of education. I could actually expand on the topics, engage and get to know the students. The staff were lovely to me and gave me everything that I needed. At the end of the week, they said I should come back if any other Maths cover work became available. One of the admin staff said a Maths role might be coming up by the end of the term, but she was not sure, so to look out for it.

To me, the school was all too clinical and heavily white, not that there was anything wrong with that, but I just could not see myself working in this type of place in the long term. Questions going through my mind were:

What would my role possibly be, apart from teaching my subject?
How could I make a difference to the students in other ways?
Would I fit in and would I be supported long-term to grow?

***

My next memorable school that I worked in, was somewhere in North London. I did a workout that day and lost probably a stone in the process. The agency called me on that morning – normally I would not take such a late booking. I liked to know more about the schools, Ofsted rating, behaviour policy, distance from home (so I can get there on time), school start and end time etc., but they convinced me.

"Shola, it's just near a main station, we will increase your daily rate." I had a sinking feeling about it, but I ignored it as she sounded desperate

"Do me this favour, Shola and I'll owe you one!"

"Ok ok, send me the details…"

First of all, it was NOT near the station, maybe 10 mins walk for an athlete, but for me, it took me about 20-25 mins. As I approached, I could see building work going on, there was a sign up to say the main entrance was closed. The agency had not mentioned this to me, so I had to walk around the site, to the new reception, two streets away. They were tearing the old school down and building a new one while still teaching in the old building as well as some lessons taking place in the new one.

Just unbelievable!

I had my nice shoes on with a bit of a heel, my briefcase and another bag with my lunch in it. If I had an egg sandwich it would have been scrambled as I was jostling with the students on the pavement, trying to make it to the reception to get briefed before the bell went.

Just thinking about it now breaks me out in a sweat. I finally get to the reception and they give me my timetable – you guessed it, spread over the two buildings and I was not just covering Maths, I was down for English and Science as well!

Then I was given a heavy computer, my cover slip and policy document – split into sections. Looking at my slip, I had lessons for the whole bloody day and was told to go straight away to complete registration for a class on the third floor! (This school is really trying to get value for money.) I literally had to pray right there and then for the good Lord to give me strength to get to the end of the day.

"You use this to get into the rooms, apart from the room you are going to now, there should be someone there to open the door for you," as she handed me a lanyard.

Yes, I could have just walked out, but I had committed, so I had to make the most of it. After all, the only ones who would suffer would be the students.

As I got upstairs, panting, sweating and struggling to hold my things, plus the damn computer, there was no other member of staff in sight to help me open the door to the room we were supposed to be in. I had approximately 30 students hovering around, already looking restless. I did not know whether to throw everything on the floor in frustration in front of the students, or to go and find someone with all of my luggage, or maybe go and hide somewhere, possibly for the rest of the day!

I could hear "We have got cover again, we have got cover again!" as the message was passed along to each student, getting louder each time.

I hadn't had time to read the policies, especially the behaviour one, but nothing in the school policy would help me out of this situation!

I took a deep breath and smiled. The kids must have thought a mad woman has arrived, I admit, I looked so dishevelled with bags hanging off each shoulder and my hands full.

"Ok, everyone quiet!" Then confidently I said, "Yes, I am covering your registration today!"

A loud cheer came from the teenagers, as they were sizing me up.

"Can someone volunteer to go and look for a member of staff with a key please, before I collapse?"

There were giggles, a slight pause, as they weighed me up. Then, a cute girl with glasses, stepped forward.

"I'll go." One of her mates was like, "Can I go with her, miss?"

I nodded and smiled with gratitude, I could not do much else in-between catching my breath.

We were told when you qualify and are teaching, you should wait at least till the end of the first term to smile, otherwise the kids will eat you alive. Well, that went out the window straight away!

And that's how I got through that day, with humour and pleas for help, and guess what, I survived but did not go back for a second day!

Shock event

Unfortunately, I got a message in December to say Filomena had passed away. I was so shocked, "What do you mean?" I kept asking. She had looked so healthy last time I saw her, as far I knew she had no underlining illness. I was devastated at the news.

Received judgement – January 2012 (approximately four months later)

The weeks turned into months. I waited to see what the conclusion was, logging on to the website to check whether my case was listed. I started to feel uneasy with how long it was taking for the written judgement; after all, the judge had partly made a judgement in my favour months ago?

I received the judgement through the post. It was 28 pages long. Reading through it quickly I initially thought it was a mistake. My paperwork had got mixed up with someone else's, surely? I had to reread and focus on the front page where the judgement was written in bold.

> It is the unanimous judgement of the tribunal that:
>
> 1. The claimant was not constructively dismissed, her claim of constructive unfair dismissal fails and is dismissed.
>
> 2. The claimant's complaints of race discrimination all fail and are dismissed.

I could not believe it! Thank God I was sitting down! Going through the judgement, Judge Prichard went on to explain away everything that had happened to me at the school, treating each incident in isolation. What more did I need to prove my case? Terms like *'very lucky'* and *'good fortune'* were used to describe Daniel and the fact he was allowed to attend the TA course and get back pay. He then went on to say,

> 'The tribunal is highly critical of the procedure that the respondents adopted whatever the policies say, it is wrong for a person specifically and personally complained about to then deal with that complaint.'

At the end, it said about me, **'it seems the claimant was just unable to accept her status as a cover supervisor'** – can you imagine! What more did I have to do to prove I was committed to the job? I was absolutely horrified! I was flabbergasted by what I was reading, were these people not in the same court room as me?

When we enquired at the court what had happened to the part that was ruled in my favour, no one seemed to know. Bizarrely, we were told eventually that the tapes or transcripts from the hearing had 'gone missing'! "What! Is someone kidding me? Is this a joke? Gone missing!" I kept repeating to myself, I was in so much shock that this could happen in a court in the UK!

We were supposed to have faith in the justice system. This ruling and the missing tapes made a mockery of it!

Even if that was the case, surely the judge should have remembered or at least written notes down to inform his final judgement. It would surely seem that some part of the judge's faculties had gone missing, as he did not even refer to his partial judgement he had made at the end of the hearing in front of me and many others in court. We had celebrated then, for crying out loud, praising him for doing the right thing, only to be let down by him months later.

Something must have happened in that four-month period for him to have so drastically changed his mind. Either way, I simply felt screwed!

"What the hell!" I kept saying to myself in frustration, I felt powerless! What the hell was I going to do now??

Slowly it dawned on me, the implications of this judgement on someone else...

"What is going to happen to Debbie now??"

***

I was so mad!

I wanted to get all the relevant people involved and go 'psycho'. Maybe, lock everyone in a room until the truth comes out like in the movies, list my demands and give them a time limit. Guess what, I would be locked away for that and the reasons why I did it would be lost in all the drama afterwards.

Maybe I should have done that on the last day of the hearing at the tribunal. If Judge Prichard had bust that move in dismissing my case, they would have no choice but to take me seriously and do the right thing.

But giving a decision in writing, months later, takes away that instinct reaction to go mad as no influential audience is present. I had left due process to unfold and now here I was, with justice denied to me.

I thought if I could have a conversation with him on my ICE app, after all it's Week 3, this is roughly how it would go.

ICE app

Judge Prichard

Ring ring

Be calm, Shola, hear him out, he might have a valid reason.

> **Me:** Afternoon, Judge Prichard, appreciate you taking my call. I know that you have had thousands of cases before you, I hope you remember the school case in 2011. Can I give you a minute to bring up the details?

A few moments go by. I try to visualise him in his home office, surrounded by luscious greenery and abundant space, I am sure. I could hear my heart was beating as I waited for his response.

FRIDAY JUNE 19TH 2020

Judge: Yes, I do remember now. Looking at the paperwork you were the black lady who wanted to be paid the same as your white counterpart, in a school, I recall?

I sighed, as it all came flooding back. Where do I start with all the questions I wanted answers to? Jumping in straightaway, I said:

Me: What happened? Why did you change your mind so dramatically from your verbal judgement in court on the final day??

Judge: Quite simply, Shola, If I had allowed one aspect through, I would have had to let the whole thing through.

Me: And what would have been wrong with that??

Judge: After the verbal judgement on the day, I realised the far-reaching implications if you had won. I won't say how many calls or conversations I got on the side afterwards, needless to say this affected my written judgement.

Me: Surely that's not fair!

Judge: Fair or not, that was my decision at the time.

Me: Even without the 'missing tapes' surely you could have looked at your written notes from the time?

Judge: I can't possibly comment on that, Shola.

There was an uncomfortable silence. In frustration, I said:

Me: Who is the head teacher accountable to then, if not the tribunal? Where do staff go to for INDEPENDENT advice or accountability if they have a dispute with a head teacher, without fear of losing their jobs?

Judge: Not absolutely sure about that…

Me: This is the problem, Judge, where do I go when I am being bullied and harassed in my workplace? I did ALL the right things expected of me and followed procedure, relying on you to do your part. I trusted the justice system and you failed me. After all, that's why equality laws were created, to be enforced by people like you, to help people like me.

Judge: You are right, sometimes the judgements we make are politically driven.

Me: You could have used this opportunity to shame Charlotte Robinson and Tom Alexander. Remember, they have the power over literally hundreds of staff daily. What do you think your judgement tells them about their behaviour, moving forward?

Judge: I didn't really take that on board at the time.

Me: As the famous saying goes 'Justice should be harsh to those who deny it to others'.

I left that to fester and moved on to another of my concerns.

Me: I think you should have taken the time before the case to learn more about the school day, timings and duties. Then you would have known more about my concerns with the work overload regarding the timetable proposed.

Judge: We just don't have the time to undertake that, I too have a heavy workload.

Yeah with a healthy pay cheque in lovely surroundings – but I didn't say that of course!

Me: I think also, you should have taken time before the case to know what the role of a cover supervisor and teacher assistant comprised of, the differences, and compare that to what I was doing.

Judge: You have a point, the panel should have put a day aside to read up and be able to have those questions answered before the trial began.

Me: I would have appreciated it if you had also looked at the other roles I was doing within the school and the value I added over the years.

Judge: Hmm... we never really got to that, maybe we should have had a more specialised panel??

Me: That would have been really helpful, as it was frustrating explaining at times. If you had the opportunity, would you review your written decision in the interest of justice?

There was a pause, I could feel he was trying to find the right wording.

Judge: Listening to the points you have put across in this conversation, Shola, and with the aftermath of George Floyd's death in conjunction with Black Lives Matter, I too have been looking at what I stand for as a privileged white judge and what I want my legacy to be. I should have used the law impartially when delivering my judgement and considered the impact it would have had on both sides. Moving forward, I will aim to enforce this with all of my fellow judges.

Me: Really!

I truly appreciate that (that took me aback, the Judge taking my points on board!).

Judge: In answer to your question, yes I would likely change my written judgement now on reflection. I apologise for any hurt it caused you. You were right, the treatment you received was totally unfair, I hope you have been able to pick up and move on with your life.

Me: It's been difficult, I must admit, but thank you, all I wanted was equality...

After I put the phone down, I felt some calm come over me. It seemed he too wanted to get things off his chest subconsciously. I had so many more questions, but I will leave for another time. Hopefully, the next discrimination case that comes in front of Judge Prichard, his judgement would simply be fair and more importantly honest.

Could I have a frank conversation on my ICE app with Stone, right now…HELL NO!!

I couldn't find the right words, not that I didn't want to, but she was not ready to talk to me. She was not ready to do the right thing…

Filomena

I had to attend her funeral to pay my respects to her even though we were not family by blood, I felt she was a part of me and was taken much too early. She will always be my 'Angel' and would be so proud of how far I have come. It was held on the 16th of January in a lovely church in Shoeburyness in Essex. The turnout was amazing, so many past students and a majority of my cohort was there. There was not a dry eye in the Church, we all went to South End Cemetery afterwards for our final goodbyes to Filomena as she was put in the ground to rest.

She would have been so proud of me and how far I had come. And she would have definitely loved my brighter wardrobe!

Just as I was getting my head around Filomena's sudden death, we heard that Whitney Houston had passed away on the 7th of February. I was distraught and in shock like many of her fans. There will never be another artist that reaches those high notes like she did, and make goose bumps break out over your skin. *'Miracle'* was one of her songs that did that to me, or perhaps she just reminded me of my youth. That movie *'Waiting to exhale'* and the soundtrack that came with it, so many tunes! It just touched a nerve about the importance of female friends, how we loved and expected to be loved.

Graduation! March 2012

I was so honoured to be finally recognised officially as a fully Qualified Maths Teacher, no one could deny or take that fact away from me!

The ceremony was to be held in one of the venues in Canterbury, Kent. I chose my outfit and paid for the ceremonial gown in advance. I was ready to go, but I nearly didn't make it.

Hubby and I were driving on the A2 motorway heading towards Canterbury with plenty of time to spare. We noticed that the temperature gauge was increasing, we looked at each other and all of a sudden smoke started coming out of the bonnet. Immediately we knew we had to pull over, we indicated and came to a halt with our hazards on.

Opening the bonnet, it became clear that the water tank had no water in. We had to wait for the engine to cool down before opening the water tank and filling it up.

We continued on our way, praying that we would get to our destination. Bearing in mind, we were behind schedule now and we couldn't drive my old banger more than 50 miles an hour or the car would have simply fallen apart. I was getting really stressed by this time because I still had to pick up my gown before the ceremony.

As we got to the outskirts of Canterbury, the gauge stated to rise again and we knew we would have to pull over a second time, but around that area were all red lines, which means:

"If you love yourself and your car, do not park here oh!" (Nigerian dialect)

We had no choice but to pull up and stop with our hazard lights on, while we gave time to allow the car to cool down. I had gotten out and was pacing up and down the road, with my lovely pristine outfit, slowly gathering dust, frantically thinking:

"How can we get to the venue on time?!" I screamed, should I and could I call a taxi? I thought, can you imagine the conversation that would follow:

"Yes, I need you to get here ASAP please!"

"No problem, Ma, where are you?"

"Well, I am around a corner from a roundabout on the outskirts of Canterbury, does that help??" (Remember, I am not a technology person, so no, I would not have downloaded an app!) I relied on my good old fashioned A-Z (for those too young to have used one, it's a physical, coloured map book) but it only covered London, which was no bloody use to me now!

I tried to flag down, anybody, to tell me exactly where I was. But, this was a predominantly white area, so it most probably would have looked like it was some sort of scam or trap to steal their vehicle. So,

FRIDAY JUNE 19TH 2020

of course they slowed down, assessed the situation and then quickly sped up and drove away in a flash.

I had left the house looking sweet, hair and nails done, skin all greased up. By the time I got back into the car my hair was frizzled and I looked as if I had just walked through the desert with all that dust on my face and clothes!

"I knew I should have taken the bloody train!" As I have done on previous occasions. This was the first time I had tried to drive it and to be honest it was much further then I had imagined. This was not the time to have experimented!

We screeched up at the venue and of course there was no parking, so we spent ages driving around. Eventually the car was dumped miles away from the venue, we literally had to sprint through back alleys, through courtyards to get there. I was wearing high heels, which I never do, so when we finally reached the venue, I was limping, my hair was all over the place and I was drenched with sweat.

I flew into the bathroom to freshen up and dashed upstairs to the changing zone, got the grown on and managed to get in the right line when my name was read out loud:

"Shola Adewale Sandy!"

I walked proudly up the ramp to the podium, ignoring the pain in my feet to collect my ribboned rolled-up paper, shook hands with the presenter, smiled and turned to the crowd, hoping Hubby would get a picture. It was over in a flash.

It was only afterwards when I was taking my picture with one of my course lecturers, Katie, that I realised with all the madness that I had lost one of my earrings! Only God knows where!

"Shola, I didn't think you were going to make it, I was looking out for you at the line-up," she said enthusiastically.

"I very nearly didn't make it," I said, as I smiled from ear to ear with relief. Being here for this ceremony was so symbolic for me, it justified everything I had been through in my mind over the last few years.

"I'm so proud of you, you are now officially a Maths teacher, you did it!"

"Thank you so much, Katie, if it wasn't for you and the team, I would not be here!"

"Cheers, Filomena." I looked up and pointed my champagne glass to the heavens, with tears of joy in my eyes, thankful she had seen my potential and given me the opportunity back then.

Beaming, I said to Katie, "Should we take a picture?" And as we posed, I made sure the shot would include the ear with the remaining earring!

Names of people that you need to have THAT conversation with:

1:

2:

3:

4:

5:

6:

7:

8:

9:

10: